Ines Scheurmann

The New Aquarium Handbook

Everything about Setting Up and Taking Care
of a Freshwater Aquarium

80 Color Photographs by Outstanding Animal
Photographers and 60 Drawings by Fritz W. Köhler

Advisory Editors: Thomas Johnson and Stephen W. Heins

BARRON'S

First English language edition published in 1986 by
Barron's Educational Series, Inc.
© 1985 by Gräfe und Unzer GmbH, Munich, West
Germany
The title of the German book is *Das GU Aquarienbuch*

Translated from the German by Helgard Niewisch, DVM

All inquiries should be addressed to:
Barron's Educational Series, Inc.
250 Wireless Blvd.
Hauppauge, NY 11788

International Standard Book No. 0-8120-3682-4
Library of Congress Catalog No. 86-7925

Library of Congress Cataloging-in-Publication Data

Scheurmann, Ines, 1950-
    The new aquarium handbook.

    Translation of: Das GU Aquarienbuch.
    Bibliography: p.
    Includes index.
    1. Aquariums, I. Title.
SF457.S3213   1985   639.3'4   86-7925
ISBN 0-8120-3682-4

PRINTED IN HONG KONG

23   490   12

Ines Scheurmann
Born in 1950, Ines Scheurmann studied biology,
specializing in the behavior of fish, and has had many
years of experience in keeping and breeding aquarium
fish. She is the author of the Gräfe and Unzer guide
Water Plants for the Aquarium and coauthor of the
Gräfe and Unzer guide *Aquariums* for beginners.

Cover Photos
Front cover: *Mesonauta festivus*.
Inside front cover: Guppies *(Poecilia reticulata)*.
Inside back cover: Diamond Tetra *(Moenkhausia
pittieri)*.
Back cover: above left: Guppy *(Poecilia reticulata)*;
above middle: Clown Loach *(Botia macracantha)*;
above right: *Synodontis multipunctatus*; middle left:
Paradisefish *(Macropodus opercularis)*; middle right:
Angelfish *(Pterophyllum scalare)*; below left: Green
Puffer *(Tetraodon fluviatilis)*; below right: *Aulonocara*
species.

A note of warning:
In this book electrical devices used in aquariums are
described. Please be sure to observe the suggestions in
the section "Safety and Other Considerations" on page
29. Otherwise serious accidents might happen.
    Before buying a large tank, check how much weight
the floor can support in the location where you plan to
set up your aquarium (see page 8).
    It is not always possible to avoid water damage
caused by broken glass, overflow, or leaks that develop
in the tank. It is therefore important to be covered by
insurance (see page 12).
    Watch out that children (and adults) do not eat
aquarium plants. Eating these plants can make people
sick. Also, keep all fish medications out of sight and
reach of children (see page 91).
    It is possible to get puncture wounds from the spines
that some species of loaches have underneath the eyes.
Since these wounds can give rise to allergic reactions,
you should immediately consult a doctor in such a
case.

Contents

Contents

Preface

An aquarium, with its brightly colored fish, beautiful plants, and caves made of rocks and stones, represents a biological life unit. When you look into an aquarium, you see an ecological system at work. It is calming, entertaining, and even exciting to watch the fish in a well-kept aquarium. There is a lot to observe—depending on the selection of fishes, the size of the tank and, especially, the familiarity of the observer with the intricacies of fish behavior.

You do not need any special talents to have an aquarium of your own; however, it is essential to have some basic knowledge about aquariums before you start to plan your tank. This includes an understanding of the chemical interaction between water, plants, and fish; an understanding of fundamental accessories; and an understanding of the different types of fish that can be kept in an aquarium and what their needs are. The goal of a successful aquarist is to create an environment that is appropriate for the specific fishes selected, which means an environment that is as close to the fishes' natural habitat as possible. *The New Aquarium Handbook* is designed to guide the aquarist along the exciting but sometimes problematic path to successfully achieving this goal. The author, Ines Scheurmann, included her personal experiences breeding and keeping tropical fish, as well as her knowledge gathered through research at the Max Planck Institute for Behavioral Physiology in Germany. She has tried to simplify the complex and voluminous information on the subject for the aquarium hobbyist. The topics addressed in this book range from setting up the tank itself to choosing tropical fishes and the right plants for various types of tanks and fish groups. Sections on nutrition, plant care, and the diseases of fish are also included, as well as information on the mechanics of aquarium accessories such as filters, heaters, and CO_2 fertilizers. Fishes and plants are individually characterized in order to allow the reader to choose the right combination to suit the individual and to match fish with environmental needs.

In a special chapter on the behavior of fish and their reproductive patterns, the author draws on her knowledge as fish-biologist to explain the fundamental life requirements of fishes and the basics for successful breeding.

The many color photos in the book will give you an idea of the variety of beautiful tropical fishes and plants available to the aquarist. The drawings will help you understand some of the mechanics involved in setting up and maintaining an aquarium; they will also help you recognize symptoms of fish diseases and some types of fish behavior, and identify a variety of aquarium plants.

The author and publisher thank all participants in the production of this book. Special thanks go to the photographers Hans Reinhard and Burkard Kahl for their outstanding color photography, and to Fritz W. Köhler for his informative drawings.

The Correct Aquarium

An aquarium is a small world in itself. Its occupants—fishes and plants—can survive in it, however, only when the aquarium owner provides the proper conditions.

The first and most important purchase is the water tank or aquarium. In addition, other equipment is necessary: a filter and aeration system tailored to the needs of the aquarium occupants, lighting, perhaps carbon dioxide (CO_2) fertilizing equipment, and—for a tropical aquarium—a heater. When purchasing a new aquarium, buy the highest quality tank and accessories you can afford. Pennies saved at this time may result in unsatisfactory equipment and continual problems and frustrations in years to come.

Types of Tanks

Frameless glass tanks (see drawing, page 6) and tanks with plastic or anodized aluminum frames have so far proved to be the most suitable. These tanks are caulked with silicone rubber. They do not rust and may therefore be used even with seawater.

Tanks with plastic insulated metal frames tend to rust after a few years' use and are not suitable for saltwater aquariums. This is also true of tanks with chrome frames.

Tanks made of acrylic are as durable as glass tanks. This plastic material can be molded into a variety of curved and semi-circular shapes. With time, however, the walls of curved acrylic tanks may belly out because of water pressure; this may also happen to rectangular or straight-walled plastic tanks. Consequently, the fish will appear somewhat distorted. Another drawback is that acrylic can be scratched more easily than glass. You may accidentally damage the walls by using a cleaning tool with a razor blade. Sand that whirls around in the tank during cleaning may also scratch the plastic.

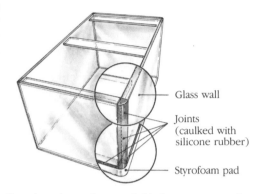
Glass wall
Joints
(caulked with
silicone rubber)
Styrofoam pad

Frameless glass tanks are suitable for many types of aquarium needs.

Small plastic tanks are excellent, however, for breeding small-fish species or as quarantine and medical treatment tanks for new and sick fish. It is advisable to buy such a small tank, 3 to 4 gallons (10 to 15 liters) in capacity, plus heater and interior filter, at the same time that you purchase your main tank. Several tanks of the same size may be stacked and stored in a relatively small space because they are narrower at the bottom than the top.

Molded one-piece glass tanks may be used for the same purposes as small plastic tanks, that is, for breeding fish and as isolation tanks when medical treatment is necessary. This type of tank is heavier than a plastic one. It can be used safely only up to about 5 gallons (20 liters) of water because of internal stress factors inherent in molded glass. Since the tank needs to be protected from sudden temperature changes and jolts, it is a good idea to set it on a Styrofoam or thick felt pad. Because chemicals affect glass less than they do plastic, an all-glass aquarium can be disinfected more easily. Therefore, when exceptional cleanliness is called for—for instance, if you want to breed delicate salmonids—a glass tank is better than a plastic one.

Caution: Should you accidentally drop your glass aquarium, do not try to catch it. Even if it breaks, you will be better off with broken glass on the floor than with serious cuts on your hands.

Size of the Tank

The size, number, and behavior patterns of the occupants determine the size of the tank. Before you purchase your new aquarium, therefore, decide on the type and number of fish you would like to have, find out to what size they will grow, and consider how much room they will require.

Use the following rule when trying to determine how much space your fish will need: 1½ to 2 quarts (liters) of water are needed per ½ inch (1 cm) of the length of a full-grown fish. The result represents just the water and does not include bottom-of-the-tank materials, decorations, and plants, which also take up space. This rule of thumb not only makes the planning of the aquarium easier, but also can be used to check overcrowding later on. Because novice aquarium hobbyists love to buy fish, overcrowding is a common mistake. It is not necessary, however, to sit glued to your aquarium, tape measure and calculator in hand, and

continuously try to figure out whether you have too many or not enough fish. The rule of thumb given above serves simply as a guide in setting up a new aquarium, and as an occasional check to prevent overpopulation. Your aquarium is not a rigid mechanical object; rather, it contains a living world. Growth, reproduction, death, and the purchase of new fish will result in continual changes.

Obviously, large fish, especially species with territorial behavior, need large aquariums. Lively endurance swimmers such as the Bala Shark *(Balantiocheilus melanopterus)* need plenty of room because they like to swim as far as possible in a straight line. Even for the small tetras, however, very small tanks are not recommended. In their native habitat these fishes live in schools of several thousands, and they want company—even in aquariums—and prefer their own kind. A small school has at least 7 to 10 fish, and they need sufficient space to swim in. For this reason the length of the aquarium should be at least 24 inches (60 cm). A school of 30 fish moving through a 30- or 36-inch (75- or 90-cm)-long aquarium (20 to 50 gallons) is an elegant sight. The same number of fish in a 16-inch (40-cm) tank (about 10 gallons) may look like an unruly crowd of children frolicking in a wading pool.

The larger the aquarium, the safer are the fish. The larger amount of water will absorb any mistakes you make more easily than would the 5 to 10 gallons (20 to 40 liters) in a small tank. When starting out, therefore, buy as large a tank as you can afford. The new owner should start out with a tank at least 24 × 16 × 12 inches (60 × 41 × 31 cm), which holds about 20 gallons (75 liters).

The Correct Aquarium

Shape of the Tank

The height of most standard-size, commercially available aquariums is greater than the front-to-back dimension. They will be adequate for most kinds of fish, but some species have special requirements. Catfishes and labyrinth fishes, for example, prefer a lower water level because they are primarily bottom and surface swimmers; they need lower and wider tanks. Large fishes, such as freshwater rays, like to burrow in the bottom sand, and therefore enjoy an aquarium with a large floor area. Fast long-distance swimmers (e.g., danios) need the widest possible tank, where they can swim long, straight stretches at a time. Such a tank is also ideal for some large species of barbs, many loaches, and some cichlids used to rapids.

Adult angelfishes and discus fishes with their large fins need the tallest and largest front-to-back tank possible to move around in freely. There would be little room for an adult angelfish to swim in if the tank had a water level of only 12 inches (30 cm). Fortunately, commercially available standard tanks are perfectly adequate for young of these species.

For some time now, tanks that have a front-to-back dimension somewhat greater than their height have been available commercially. It is advisable to go with that shape. Although standard tanks fit in with modern furniture and offer a large viewing surface, an aquarium with a greater front-to-back dimension is roomier and more versatile. The greater the floor area of an aquarium, the healthier are its occupants—both fish and plants. A large floor area offers a good opportunity for decorating and for arranging plants. Another advantage of a tank with the shape suggested above is that fishes with territorial behavior can stake out their territories. Also, lighting is more effective.

Tanks of special size or shape must be custom-made either by a commercial manufacturer or by the aquarium hobbyist himself.

Weight of the Tank

Apart from the needs of the fish and plants, you must consider also the weight of the aquarium when it is filled with water. Its weight is determined by its capacity, which is calculated by using the following formula:*

$$\text{Capacity (in gallons)} = \frac{\text{length} \times \text{width} \times \text{height (in inches)}}{231}$$

Since 1 gallon of water weighs over 8 pounds, an aquarium measuring about 48 × 13 × 20 inches holds about 55 gallons and weighs approximately 460 pounds (210 kg). Add about one quarter of this figure for the weight of the tank, bottom material, and decorations. In the above example, the finished aquarium would

---

*With metric measurements, the formula would be:

$$\text{Capacity (in liters)} = \frac{\text{length} \times \text{width} \times \text{height (in cm)}}{1000}$$

Since 1 liter of water weighs 1 kilogram, an aquarium measuring 100 × 40 × 50 cm holds 200 liters and weighs 200 kg. The filled aquarium would weigh about 250 kg.

Catfishes and tetras.
Above: Fat Fin Catfish (*Pimelodus* species); below: Congo Tetra (*Phenacogrammus interruptus*).

weigh about 600 pounds (270 kg). This does not include the weight of the stand on which the tank rests or the filter.

Some floors cannot support more than 300 pounds (140 kg) of weight per square yard (meter).

Important: If you are planning on a large aquarium, consult an architect or builder to find out exactly how much weight your floor can safely support.

The Tank Cover

Most aquariums should be covered at the top with a piece of glass or plastic to keep dust out and prevent fish from escaping. The cover should be strong enough to resist breaking if, for example, children throw some of their toys on top, and should have one or more openings for filter and heater tubing, and for feeding the fish.

The cover may be cut into several individual panels made to fit the tank exactly. That way you do not have to lift the entire cover every time you want to feed the fish. Individual panels also make it easier to clean the cover. Plastic runners are available in which the panels may be easily moved as needed. (Of special help are handles made of glass or plastic and glued on with silicone rubber, which make it easier to move the panels back and forth.) Make sure that the cover does not provide an airtight barrier, and also that the cracks between the panels are not large enough for fish to squeeze through.

If you are using an aquarium cover with special built-in lighting, you will not need a standard cover.

Correct Location and Base

Thanks to modern lighting methods, you no longer need to place the tank by the window, as was required years ago. Actually, a window makes a poor location: sunlight fosters the growth of algae and raises the water temperature to the point where it is no longer suitable for fish. For instance, in a southern exposure, summer heat may increase the water temperature to about 105°F (40°C), whereas most tropical fish tolerate only about 85°F (30°C) at best. If a window is the only possible location, make sure to shield the side of the tank facing the window with a thick Styrofoam panel to protect it from sunlight. For lighting choose a lamp that comes with a built-in complete aquarium cover. If the tank has to be near any kind of heater, you must also protect the side facing the heat source with a Styrofoam panel.

If possible, choose a location near one or more electrical outlets. If you plan to use more than one tank, you may want to consider placing them close to a faucet and sink.

Make sure that the floor is absolutely level. If you find that the floor slants, you will need to even it out. Any base on which the aquarium will rest (tabletop, stand, shelf, etc.) must be perfectly stable and

Tetras.
Above left: X-ray Fish *(Pristella riddlei)*; above right: Cardinal Tetra *(Cheirodon axelrodi)*; middle left: Penguin Fish *(Thayeria boehlkei)*; middle right: Red or Striped Headstander *(Anostomus anostomus)*; below left: False Rummy-nosed Tetra *(Petitella georgiae)*; below right: Marbled Hatchetfish *(Carnegiella strigata strigata)*.

level in order not to bend under the weight of a full aquarium. Since some tanks may develop breaks or leaks, you had better place a layer of Styrofoam or felt under your aquarium.

Small tanks may be placed on a table or shelf. A larger one needs a strong, stable base, such as a brick-type stand or other pedestal-base, sturdy enough to carry the weight. Do not buy a flimsy base—water is *very* heavy!

Wooden insulation around the aquarium saves energy because heat from the tank and lamps remains trapped for a longer period. You can probably find commercially available a chest (with base) with a built-in aquarium and all accessories. Such "furniture" comes in a variety of sizes and styles and may be matched to most home decorating schemes. Of course, if you are handy with tools you can build your own version, incorporating ample space for both tank and accessories. The interior of the cover needs to be perfectly water-proof. Waterproofing may be achieved by applying either liquid plastic or plastic panels. Interior seams must be sealed with silicone rubber to keep all wood surfaces free of water. Because some manufacturers offer unsealed aquarium chests, even commercially purchased "furniture" may need to be sealed and waterproofed before use.

Rental/Lease Contracts and Insurance Against Damage

It is important that you check your rental/lease contracts and consult with your landlord and insurance carrier before purchasing an aquarium. You need, first, to know whether you have permission to keep an aquarium and, second, to consider potential problems arising from damage as a result of maintaining an aquarium, such as broken glass, leaks, and overflow.

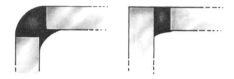

Corner joints for rectangular glass tanks. Left: Most popular joint shape, suitable for both large and small tanks. Right: Dull-short joint, suitable only for tanks that are less than 30 inches (80 cm) in length.

Corner joints for tanks with 5 or more corners. Left: Joint for oblique-cut glass panes. Right: Joint for regular pane angles.

Repairing a Tank

A glass tank needs to be handled with the same care as any other object of glass. Nevertheless, despite every precaution, glass may break—for example, during a move. If the break occurs in a glass tank that has been sealed with silicone rubber, any expert dealing with glass may be able to recommend an appropriate repair shop. Before taking the tank for repair, carefully loosen any broken glass by using a sharp knife or similar tool along the sealed edges. Wear sturdy work gloves, and use special care not to cut yourself. When transporting the tank, avoid injury or damage by taping all remaining sharp edges with thick layers of newspaper or foam rubber. Leave everything else to the expert.

Do not expect to take your aquarium home immediately, even if you were able to watch its repair. All grooves and joints need to harden and set first. When the expert has released the tank—that is, when everything has dried and set sufficiently— check to make sure that the tank is really waterproof. Fill it with water and let it sit a while before inserting decorations and plants. Also, it is a good idea to clean the inside thoroughly with a solution of sodium bicarbonate in order to neutralize any remaining traces of acetic acid, which is contained in silicone rubber.

Sometimes the same repairman who has the expertise to restore your tank may also be able to construct a special setup for an aquarium (see drawing, page 13).

Types of Aquariums

It is not an easy task to separate the various types of aquariums. For example, a community aquarium may also represent a plant aquarium, and a species aquarium may also serve as a breeding aquarium. Nevertheless, there are some definite differences.

Community Aquarium

A community aquarium contains fishes and plants that thrive under similar conditions in their native habitats, even though they may originate in different continents. A community tank may contain South American tetras and catfishes, as well as Southeast Asian barbs and West African cichlids. If fishes and plants from a variety of habitats

are to live harmoniously, they need to complement each other in terms of requiring similar water, temperature, and lighting conditions. They must be compatible and present no potential danger to each other. Neither fishes nor plants will thrive, and illnesses will quickly follow, if a hodgepodge variety of fish species is put into a tank without regard for individual habits and needs.

In setting up a community aquarium, the needs of its occupants, rather than their shapes and colors, constitute the most important factor. Plants used to soft water will not thrive if they are forced to share the tank with plants that need hard water. Red Swordtails offer a striking contrast to angelfishes, but the two differ substantially in their water-quality requirements. Red neons are most decorative

L-shaped aquarium designed to fit into the corner of a room. This type of tank must be custom made; it can be ordered through aquarium stores.

and have the same environmental needs as angelfishes with respect to water and temperature. Unfortunately, however, angelfishes consider the neons delectable little morsels and like to make them their main food. Therefore, if you take the time and trouble to learn a little about the requirements of various fishes and plants, you will be better able to set up a community tank in which all the occupants live well together.

If you want to avoid competition among the various fishes, you may want to fill your aquarium with species that have different habits. For example, top and bottom feeders can usually live in peace together. As a rule, fishes needing hiding places are compatible with those that swim about freely in the tank. Plant eaters usually live well with carnivores.

In short, there is a lot to learn before setting up a community aquarium. A beginner, in particular, should learn as much as possible about the individual needs of the tank's future occupants, because a novice usually starts out with a community aquarium.

An efficient filtering system is the most important equipment for a community aquarium. The water has to be kept as clean as possible to compensate for the fact that the particular needs of all the different species of fish cannot be perfectly met.

Species Aquarium

In a species aquarium there is only one species of fish. Interior decorations and plants, water conditions, and food are tailored as closely as possible to the needs of the species. A species aquarium is best for groups of fishes that have needs and habits radically different from those of other species. Such an aquarium is suitable for the voracious snakeheads, the quarrelsome breeding cichlid parents, or the small and delicate dwarf carps. Other species aquariums may contain fishes that have adapted to extremely hard or soft water, such as fishes from desert areas or from brackish waters.

If you would like to breed and observe certain species because of their intriguing breeding habits, you would need to put such fishes in a special species aquarium. In a community aquarium, fish may be unable to spawn or their fry may be eaten. A species aquarium therefore often serves also as a breeding aquarium.

Breeding Aquarium

One of the most exciting (and important) undertakings of an aquarium hobbyist is the breeding of fish. Catfishes, cichlids, and similar species are generally bred in the same aquarium in which they are kept, that is, the species aquarium. They take care of their eggs themselves, defend their spawn against attacks from their own kind, and protect their young.

With a species that does not take care of its young, you will need a special breeding tank. For successful spawning, most tetras and many barbs and other cyprinids need mineral-poor, acidic water that may also have to be filtered over peat. Such water is not suitable in a fully planted community or species aquarium, since the water is not pH-buffered, and plants will not grow. In addition, rocks and bottom materials are not conducive

The Correct Aquarium

to the kind of water—clean and free of bacteria—that is necessary for breeding. Have on hand small species tanks, either glass or plastic, which have been disinfected and filled with soft water from an ion-exchanger. Then add the desired species, either in pairs or in small groups. Remove the adult fish immediately after spawning.

A breeding aquarium needs a heater, filter, and lighting appropriate to the size of the tank. You may find small ion-exchangers on the market that function as filters and keep the water soft and acidic.

Paint the outside of the bottom of the tank black to keep it from reflecting. This is necessary for sanitary reasons because breeding aquariums usually lack bottom materials that would absorb reflected light, thereby preventing it from stimulating unwanted algal and bacterial growth. Also, cover the bottom with glass marbles or small glass rods, so that when the eggs sink to the bottom they well out of the reach of voracious parents. Artificial plantlike spawning webs are available for species that need plants for spawning.

To raise the young, transfer either the eggs or the small fry into a larger tank. The rearing tank needs a more efficient filter because the young brood requries optimal water conditions.

Dutch (Plant) Aquarium

The so-called Dutch aquariums represent primarily community tanks for plants. One might call them botanical underwater gardens. Until recently, only the Dutch seemed to know how to establish such a tank properly, and that is how these aquar-

Large aquarium—about 4½ feet (150 cm) in length—is stocked with East African cichlids. A decorative wooden enclosure was necessary to hide essential equipment (a large external filter and the heater).

The Correct Aquarium

iums got their name. It so happens that in many regions of Holland the water is soft and slightly acidic, whereas much of Europe and North America has hard or medium-hard water. In recent years, however, changes have taken place: ion-exchangers have become less expensive, carbon dioxide diffusers and mercury vapor lamps have appeared on the market, and an excellent fertilizer for bottom plants has become commercially available. In short, every hobbyist who chooses to do so can now set up a strikingly beautiful plant aquarium.

In addition to the plant fertilizer (check commercial products with your dealer), a bottom-heating system, such as a mat or cable, is important equipment when setting up this type of aquarium. Plants must have a well-aerated bottom, and their roots must not get chilled.

An ion-exchanger or peat filtering system is necessary to treat the water because the most beautiful water plants, such as *Cryptocoryne affinis, Cabomba caroliniana, Rotala macrandra,* and *Hygrophila,* prefer soft, somewhat acidic water. Carbon dioxide fertilizing (see page 59) and bright lighting are also essential.

Only the small and delicate tetras, barbs, and other cyprinids, algae-eating fishes, and perhaps some small catfishes are suitable for a Dutch aquarium. Arrange plants according to their decorative beauty only; forget about their geographic origins. Achieve contrasting effects by planting each group with size, shape, and color in mind. The finished product should always give the impression of a well-tended garden, and that means avoiding overgrowth and other evidence of neglect.

Goldfish Aquarium

Unfortunately, many unsuitable glass containers for goldfish are commercially available. A proper habitat for goldfish is a pond or a very large tank 30 to 40 inches (80 to 100 cm) in length. Instead, these fish are forced into containers that are much too small and in which they may just barely exist for years. Goldfish grow very rapidly, they need a lot of food, and they excrete large amounts of waste products

In a large tank, excreta are usually quickly filtered out or used up by plants. In a glass bowl, however, these waste products will transform clean water into a smelly mess within 2 days. The goldfish then lack a stable environment because the water has to be changed constantly. Plants could absorb part of the nitrogenous substances, but because goldfish like to burrow and poke around the bottom, plants will not last in such a small container.

The need to provide enough oxygen and to remove carbon dioxide further complicates matters. This exchange of gases occurs quickly and efficiently in an aquarium with a large water surface. A small glass container, however, has a surface that is inadequate. In a standard aquarium carbon dioxide is removed through ventilation, but the narrow opening at the top of a goldfish bowl prevents the carbon dioxide from escaping. It will form a thick layer right above the water surface, so that the intake of oxygen and the escape of carbon dioxide become slower. The goldfish are constantly near death from suffocation. It is sheer cruelty to keep goldfish in a small glass bowl.

If you want to keep goldfish, provide them with the same type of environment you would give any tropical species.

Water—The Natural Environment of Fish

The survival of fish and plants depends largely on the quality of the water. It is entirely up to the aquarium hobbyist whether the fish will thrive in clean, fresh water in which breathing is easy or whether they will eke out a pitiful existence in dirty, neglected water. The water in an aquarium must be checked regularly. Your dealer will show you the many tools available to help you check the water. They are easy to handle and simple to understand and use—even a novice can do things right the first time!

It is imperative that the aquarium hobbyist really understand the basic processes occurring, and the potential water-quality problems that may arise, in the water of an aquarium. Being well informed helps you utilize all possible opportunities to do things right.

Not all water is alike. In nature there is no such thing as chemically pure water. Any water occurring naturally contains dissolved gases, minerals, and organic matter from leaves, decaying wood, and living and dead organisms.

Gases Dissolved in Water

Oxygen and carbon dioxide (CO_2) are essential for all occupants of an aquarium. Fish and plants both take up oxygen and give off carbon dioxide when they breathe. Water absorbs oxygen from the air (and from plants; see below). Maximum absorption occurs when the movement of water at the surface is strongest. It follows that a rapidly moving stream is much richer in oxygen than a stagnant pond. Also, cold water absorbs oxygen better than warm water: water at a temperature of 32°F (0°C) contains twice as much oxygen as water at 86°F (30°C). Cold-water fishes generally need much more oxygen than do warm-water fishes, which have adapted to the lower oxygen of their environments.

Fish tend to stay suspended at the water surface and gasp for air if there is not enough oxygen available. It will do no immediate good to increase aeration, because it takes time for the water to absorb enough oxygen. Rather, you need to give first aid by adding a commercially available oxygen product (check with your dealer). Before adding this product, however, remove some of the water for quick analysis, because the same symptoms of distress can also occur from an excess of carbon dioxide or from ammonia, nitrate, or nitrite poisoning. Be very conservative in your use of oxygen products: water supersaturated with oxygen can harm some species of fish.

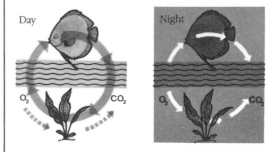

Oxygen and carbon dioxide exchange between fish and plants. During the day: Fish inhale oxygen (O_2) and exhale carbon dioxide (CO_2). Plants take up CO_2 and produce O_2 through the process of photosynthesis. At night (or with low illumination): Plants as well as fish use O_2 and produce CO_2. Photosynthesis is not possible when it is dark.

Water—The Natural Environment of Fish

The oxygen contained in the water not only originates in the air but also is produced by plants during the process of photosynthesis. They take up carbon dioxide in order to make organic matter, producing oxygen as a by-product. Aquatic plants get carbon dioxide from the water around them. Part of the CO_2 comes from the air, part from the fish and other plants. Carbon dioxide exists in the water as carbonic acid (dissolved CO_2, bicarbonate, and carbonate).

Carbon dioxide is relatively abundant in natural waters. Our drinking water, however, contains very little CO_2, so that plants frequently need additional fertilizing (see Carbon Dioxide Fertilizing, page 59).

On the other hand, an aquarium may show signs of excessive carbon dioxide. In that case the water is saturated with CO_2 exhaled by the fish. In such water a fish is no longer able to exhale CO_2. Therefore excessive CO_2 must be removed, and this can be accomplished quickly by inducing strong, rapid water movement—for example, by means of an airstone (see page 41). A modest level of aeration, however, will prevent the build-up of CO_2.

Your dealer may be able to show you helpful accessories to measure the concentration of carbon dioxide in the water. Better yet, keep in mind the requirements of fish and plants when you first purchase your equipment and set up your aquarium. It is much simpler to do things right from the beginning than to try to remedy problems later on. If your aquarium has many plants but few fish, very little water movement is required, but a fairly tight cover is needed to retain the CO_2 in the water and keep it available for the plants. The plants in turn will then give off sufficient oxygen for the fish. On the other hand, a lot of water movement and turnover will be required if the tank has few or no plants. In this case the CO_2 must be removed from the water, and the aquarium should not be covered tightly.

Aeration is also needed in a community tank, which, although it may contain plants, may at the same time be hopelessly overcrowded and poorly lighted. Such a tank contains too many oxygen consumers and carbon dioxide manufacturers.

Hardness of the Water

In nature, water normally contains variable amounts of calcium and magnesium salts. These salts are important when determining the hardness of water. Water is considered hard if it contains a large amount of such salts and soft if it has only a little.

A "dH" scale expresses the hardness of water in degrees. Each degree corresponds to 30 milligrams of calcium carbonate per 1 quart (liter) of water. The dH scale is not widely used outside of Europe. Other scales may be employed by manufacturers of kits for testing water hardness.

    0–4 dH = very soft
    5–8 dH = soft
    9–12 dH = medium hard
    13–20 dH = hard
    20 dH = very hard

Since the soils in the native habitats of aquarium fishes contain little or no calcium, these fishes have adapted to soft and often very soft water. Only some East African cichlids and some fishes from temperate

Freshwater Butterfly Fish (*Pantodon buchholzi*).

18

Water—The Natural Environment of Fish

climates live in a natural environment of medium-hard to hard water.

Your local water department can tell you the degree of hardness of your tap water, or you can check it yourself by using either a special test kit purchased from your dealer or an electronic measuring device (see page 42). Cities and other heavily populated areas are often connected to additional water supplies. When demand increases, water companies may have to supplement local water with water from a different area and of a different hardness and chemical composition. At times, therefore, your tap water may vary quite suddenly in its degree of hardness, and you should check it from time to time.

The total hardness represents a combination of carbonate and noncarbonate salts of calcium and magnesium. Boiling reduces hardness by precipitating calcium and magnesium. Carbonate hardness should be low for fish used to soft water. If it is too high, minerals must be removed from the water, either by boiling or with an ion-exchanger. Noncarbonate, or "permanent," hardness is less important when dealing with aquarium fish. You need to check the degree of total hardness with a test kit or other measuring device (see page 25).

If you would like to keep fishes other than those adapted to the hardness of the water in your particular area, you will need to soften or harden the water for your aquarium. City water is almost always harder than natural tropical waters. You can soften your water by buying distilled water to mix with it, but this can become expensive for large quantities of water. Rainwater is no longer suitable for aquarium use because of heavy pollution in recent years. For large volumes of water the only solution may be to buy an ion-exchanger (water-softening filter) that removes minerals from the water and generally regulates the chemical composition of the water. Which of the many types of ion-exchangers you should purchase will depend on the particular mineral components and the ionic strength of your tap water (see page 26). A number of water-softening resins and chemicals are available.

Occasionally you may want to make soft water harder. That will be the case, for example, if your tap water is very soft, but you want to keep live-bearing toothed carps or large cichlids from lakes Malawi and Tanganyika. To harden water, you can use gypsum, but not the type you patch walls with. Buy the pure alabaster gypsum available in pet stores, and follow product instructions carefully.

For more in-depth information about degrees of hardness of water, ion-exchangers, and adding or removing minerals from water, consult experts such as aquarium dealers or the literature dealing with water chemistry in aquariums.

Carps.
Above left: Minnow *(Phoxinus phoxinus)*; above right: White Cloud *(Tanichthys albonubes)*; middle left: Red-tailed "Shark" *(Labeo bicolor)*; middle right: Banded Loach *(Botia hymenophysa)*; below left: Coolie Loach or Leopard Eel *(Acanthophthalmus kuhlii)*; below right: Dwarf Loach *(Botia sidthimunki)*.

Acidity of the Water

The acidity of water is just as important as its degree of hardness. All natural water contains a certain amount of substances that act as either acids or alkalis. Water is said to be acid if it contains more acids than alkalis, and to be alkaline if it contains more alkalis than acids. If acid and alkaline substances are present in equal amounts, water is said to be chemically neutral. (Chemically pure water contains neither acid nor alkaline substances and is thus neutral.)

The acidity of water is expressed in pH units on a scale of 1 to 14. Neutral water has a pH of 7. Water is acid if its pH value is below 7, and is alkaline if above 7. Water thus becomes more acid or alkaline the further its pH value moves away from 7.

A water pH of 5.8 to 7 is suitable for most tropical fish. Only cichlids from East African lakes have adapted to alkaline water; they need water with a pH of 7.5 to 8.5. Since fish will show signs of acid or alkaline damage at pH values below 5.5 and above 9, a regular pH check of your aquarium water is mandatory. The pH values can be measured with electrical pH-meters or with the easy-to-use test kits widely available at pet stores. You may be able to obtain indicator strips accurate enough for aquarium purposes (pH range 6 to 8, sensitivity 0.2 pH unit); if so, these are a quick and convenient, although costly, method.

Buffers that you can add to adjust pH are inexpensive and readily available at aquarium stores. Use sodium biphosphate to lower pH; sodium bicarbonate to raise it.

Humic Acid and Peat

The native waters of our aquarium fishes are made acid by carbonic acid and organic humic acid. The latter is formed by decay-

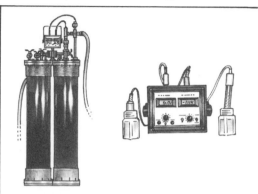

Left: Ion-exchanger for softening water. Right: Combination instrument that measures both pH and conductivity of water.

ing leaves, wood, and other plant materials. Humic acid helps prepare nutrients for water plants.

Water in tropical areas has considerably higher levels of humic acid than carbonic acid. The highest levels of humic acid are found in the black-water rivers of the Amazon basin and in some West African rivers, where the pH of the water can be below 4. Fish and plants in tropical regions have adapted to humic-acidic water and therefore need additional humic acid in aquariums. This can be supplied either by circulating the water through a peat filter (see page 36) or by adding liquid peat extract.

Tannin substances in peat and peat extracts tend to harden the skin of fish, and therefore parasitic single-cell organisms and fungi cannot easily adhere to it. You must remember, however, not to add too much peat extract to breeding tanks designed for black-water fishes. The tannin may harden the eggshells to such an extent that the larvae, unable to crack the shells, wil die in their eggs.

Water—The Natural Environment of Fish

Molarity and Salt Concentration

Most tropical fish require low carbonate hardness, but other salts in solution are also of importance. Salts, either in the water or in plant and animal cells, draw water through cell membranes—a phenomenon called *osmosis*. Fish are in osmotic balance with their natural environments, but are often unable to handle water with a different salinity. With freshwater fishes, a high salt concentration in the water draws water from the organism, thereby upsetting its normal physiology. Saltwater fishes are adjusted to high salt concentrations, but cannot tolerate fresh water because they cannot control the influx of water caused by the salt in their cells.

Individual cells such as eggs and sperm tend to be more sensitive to osmotic conditions than is the whole animal. This can be critical, since fertilization takes place in the water. For example, if a fish adapted to soft water deposits its eggs in hard water, the eggs will shrivel up as they lose water to the high-salinity of the water around them. The reverse—too little salt in the water—is just as bad for eggs and sperm.

Therefore, you must be very conscientious about water quality if you want to breed fish. The aquarium water should be as close as possible in composition to the native water. You should know the salt content of your water. Have your water tested, or purchase a conductivity meter, which measures the electrical conductivity of the water. More salts mean higher electrical conductivity. Many pet and aquarium stores sell several types of instruments, to measure water conductivity.

Nitrogen Compounds

In the native habitats of all aquarium fishes nitrogen compounds are relatively rare. An aquarium, however, that is always overpopulated relative to the natural habitat may contain too much of the various nitrogen compounds.

Fish excrete ammonia with their urine and feces. Decaying proteins—leftover food, dead snails, dead fish, decomposing leaves—also produce ammonia. If you tend to overfeed your fish, you may be the main cause of excess ammonia because unused food will keep decomposing at the bottom of the tank. Ammonia is poisonous even at low concentrations. Luckily, the slightly acid water that most fish prefer converts ammonia into ammonium, which is much less toxic. Unfortunately, this process is reversible; alkaline water converts ammonium to the highly toxic ammonia.

As long as the pH of the water remains somewhat on the acid side, between about 5.8 and 7, fish can live even in the large amounts of debris contained in an aquarium that has been neglected for months. If the water is circulated through an acid-enhancing filter material such as peat, the ammonia will be converted to ammonium, and the fish will survive. But if the aquarium hobbyist suddenly decides to take care of the long overdue change of water, and replaces about one-third of the water with tap water, he may be surprised. Since tap water is usually on the alkaline side, the pH in the aquarium rises. As a result the ammonium changes to ammonia, and the fish die of ammonia poisoning.

Before these interconnections were properly understood, it was assumed (and some people still think) that fish living in acid water could not tolerate a change. Sometimes water was not changed for years on end. Every drop of "old" water was carefully saved. Back then, certain devices were invented—some are still available today—that would remove the debris but not the water. Some aquarium hobbyists possessed enough sensitivity and intuition to keep their fish alive for decades despite these conditions and were even able to breed fish. They managed this feat, however, only when they kept just a few fish, did not overfeed them, and had set up a well-planted aquarium, in which the plants used up the ammonium present in the water.

Today, when we speak of "aged water," we mean water that has been in a tank without fish, but with plants, for several weeks and is now of a quality to provide a healthy environment for fish. "Fresh water" means tap water that has sat for some time.

Cichlids from East African lakes are used to alkaline water. If they are forced to live in dirty aquarium water, they face the constant danger of ammonia poisoning. These fish are heavy feeders and usually nip off the plants in the tank. Therefore, an especially powerful filter is necessary, and the water must be changed more often than for other fishes.

A filter converts ammonia and ammonium first into nitrites and then into nitrates. Bacteria of the genus *Nitrosomonas* help in the conversion to nitrite, which is as toxic as ammonia. Guppies *(Poecilia reticulata),* which are often recommended as the first fish for the novice because they are considered hardy, will tolerate up to 1 mg mitrite per quart (liter) of water.

Since most other species have far less tolerance for nitrites, it is important that the latter be converted to nitrates as quickly as possible. Bacteria of the genus *Nitrobacter* accomplish this change. Nitrate is a relatively innocuous nitrogen compound, although it may be harmful at levels of 150 mg nitrite per quart (liter) of water. should not be permitted to accumulate in an aquarium. Tap water usually contains more nitrate than do tropical waters, and too much nitrate damages plants by causing rotting due to *Cryptocoryne* species.

The transformation of ammonia/ammonium into nitrite and nitrate uses up a lot of oxygen. If an aquarium is overcrowded, its water is low in oxygen, and it contains debris and leftover food, bacteria tend to do their work at a much slower pace and may even stop working altogether. The result is an accumulation of ammonia or nitrite in the water. With a severe lack of oxygen, bacteria may even convert nitrate to nitrite or even back to ammonia/ammonium in order to regain oxygen. This process may occur in the water or even in the fish themselves. The fish then suffer from nitrite poisoning. Nitrite attaches to the red blood cells, and body tissues are no longer able to absorb oxygen. The symptoms of nitrite poisoning are the same as those of oxygen deficiency, excessive carbon dioxide, and ammonia poisoning: the fish come to the surface and gasp for air. If that happens, immediately remove about 1 quart (liter) of water for testing, add some oxygen tablets to the water to save the fish, and then check to find out exactly what is the problem. Chemicals available at aquarium stores will remove ammonia. If you are dealing with nitrite poisoning, you may no longer be

Water—The Natural Environment of Fish

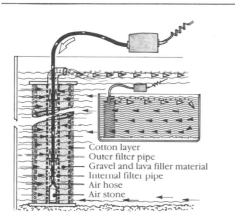

— Cotton layer
— Outer filter pipe
— Gravel and lava filler material
— Internal filter pipe
— Air hose
— Air stone

Biological inside filter. Water is forced through the entire filter membrane surface, then pushed up by the bubbling air. The water current is light or strong, depending on the force of the pump.

able to measure the presence of this compound. Bacteria may have converted it meanwhile either to ammonia/ammonium or back again to nitrate. The nitrite remains in the fish themselves, however, and is lethal.

You can easily prevent this unpleasant situation by changing the aquarium water regularly. Plants are also helpful in removing troublesome compounds; all plants prefer to take up ammonium rather than nitrate. Plants like *Lemna,* the floating fern *Ceratopteris,* and *Eichhornia* do a thorough job of clearing the water. They take up oxygen from the air, rather than the water as aquarium plants normally do, and therefore do not compete with the fish, even in the dark. You can also use common houseplants to keep the water clean. Set a few airroots of *Philodendron* in your aquarium; they will branch out and clear the water of unwanted harmful substances.

The quantity and types of plants and fish determine the frequency with which the water in the aquarium should be changed. Check the water about every 2 weeks for its nitrite and nitrate levels. An easy way to check for nitrite is to smell the water; too much nitrite makes water smell bad.

The *Nitrosomonas* and *Nitrobacter* bacteria active in the formation of nitrite and nitrate, respectively, are not present in sufficient amounts in a newly set up aquarium. It will take a few weeks to establish a fully functioning bacteria population. Although you may be able to shorten the process by transferring some filter material or bottom materials from an already established aquarium onto the filter of your new aquarium, you will run the risk of introducing diseases into your new aquarium. You will be better off to keep just a few fish in your tank at first and to feed them lightly during this initial time period.

Remember that an adequate number of filter bacteria have to operate at all times. Never clean a filter at the same time you are working on a major change of water. Wait a minimum of 1 week after a water change to clean the filter.

Measuring Equipment and Reagents

You can find all necessary instruments and chemicals for water care in any aquarium specialty store. Reagents to test pH and hardness can be bought individually, or packaged for multiple purposes.

Electrical measuring devices are available, although not at all common in the United States, and newly developed electronic

Water—The Natural Environment of Fish

versions accommodate large aquariums. Such devices measure everything from salt concentrations to pH, hardness, temperature, oxygen, and CO_2 levels. Newer models incorporate a complete, balanced maintenance program for the water, including all chemical requirements. A 20-gallon tank does not require this type of sophisticated equipment. If, however, you are planning to keep several sensitive species of fish, where constant water exchange and requirements are critical, you should balance the convenience and efficiency of these very expensive instruments against the long-term costs of manual measurements with individual reagents.

From Tap Water to Aquarium Water

Our tap water is designed for human consumption. It contains no carbonic acid and no carbon dioxide, and many important plant nutrients such as phosphates, iron, and manganese have been removed from it.

Sometimes our water contains traces of toxic substances due to pollution and traces of heavy metals. Obviously, tap water is a poor environment for delicate fishes such as dwarf cichlids and some imported species. You will need to remove potentially toxic substances and provide the proper conditions before adding these fishes. (Useful products for this purpose can be found at your local aquarium shop.) You also have to remember to fertilize your plants.

A new aquarium should be "dry run" for about 2 to 3 weeks; that is, it should be set up, filled with water, and planted, and all equipment, such as the filter and air pump, should be turned on—all this without fish in the tank. In this way plants have time to grow roots, filter bacteria can develop fully, and the tap water will turn into suitable aquarium water.

The Native Waters of Aquarium Fishes

The following section describes types of water from several different regions, taken at various times of the year. Not included are seasonal fluctuations in mineral content and pH. Also, the descriptions do not reflect geological differences in the native countries of the various aquarium fishes.

Nevertheless, this overview of various water conditions in nature provides some helpful rules of thumb for aquarium owners. If you just want to keep aquarium fishes, you can easily provide suitable water that is either harder or softer, more acid or more alkaline, than they are used to. The fishes will do well as long as the water is clean. But if you want to breed your aquarium fishes successfully, you must provide water with the same mineral content and pH as the native waters to which the various species adapted over millions of years.

South America

For the aquarium hobbyist, the Amazon region is the most fascinating area of South America. It is the home of some of the most common and most colorful aquarium fishes, such as the Neon Tetra, discus fishes, angelfishes, armored catfishes, and dwarf cichlids.

Three types of water occur in the rivers of this region:

White water, found in the main branch of the Amazon River, for instance, is yellow, clayey, and very murky. This water is soft

(0.6 to 1.2 dH) and slightly acid (pH 6.5 to 6.9), with only minute traces of ammonium and nitrate.

Clear water is transparent and yellow to dark olive green in color. It is extremely soft (0.3 to 0.8 dH) and somewhat more acidic than "white water" (pH 4.6 to 6.6). It contains only traces of ammonium and nitrate.

Black water, found in the Rio Negro, is quite transparent and is dark brown. It is even softer (0 to 0.1 dH) and more acid (pH 3.8 to 5.3) than "clear water." It has hardly any ammonium and nitrate.

There is of course no clear dividing line between these different water types. Most of our decorative tropical fishes come from areas where black water mixes with clear water or white water.

Central America

This is the home of the live-bearing toothed carps. These fishes live in medium-hard to hard water that is neutral or slightly alkaline. Some are also found in brackish water.

Most Central American cichlids live in slightly softer water. In the mountainous interior areas the water is soft to very soft and slightly acid. It would not be a good idea to keep these cichlids together with swordtails or other live-bearing fishes in the same "Central American" tank.

North America

Sun perches (Centrarchidae) and catfishes (Ictaluridae) live in North American waters. They prefer slightly cooler water than do tropical fish. Most of these species can be found in many areas of North America and in a variety of types of water. In an aquarium they may be kept in medium-hard to hard water with a neutral pH (pH 7).

Africa

Many egg-laying cyprinodonts (they prefer water somewhat higher in mineral content), characins, and cichlids are found in West Africa. The rivers of western and central Africa are generally low in mineral content, and slightly acid. Stanley Pool, Zaire, for example, has a hardness of 2.0 dH, a pH of 6.5, and almost no ammonium and nitrate. Some of these areas have water that is even softer and more acid.

The East African lakes, primarily Lakes Tanganyika and Malawi, are the native habitats of many mouthbreeding cichlids. They live in harder, alkaline waters; Lake Tanganyika, for example, has water of about 10 dH and a pH of 7.5 to 9.2. They are usually bred in aquarium water with a hardness of 17.0 dH and a pH of 8.2. They can tolerate even harder water.

Southeast Asia

The danios are found in southern India and Sri Lanka. The water in these regions is very soft (0.2 to 0.7 dH) and practically neutral. The Malayan Archipelago is the home of most of our aquarium fishes other than those from South America. The Rasbora, or Harlequin Fish, the Sumatra barbs, and many types of loaches can be found here. The water contains practically no minerals and is quite clean. It has a dH of 0.6 and a pH of 6.0.

Europe

European fishes small enough for an aquarium are generally quite adaptable and can be kept in medium-hard to hard water of 10 to 15 and even 20 dH and a pH near 7. Egg-laying toothed carps from southern Europe (Cyprinodontidae) need medium-hard water of 8 to 10 dH and a pH near 7.

Aquarium Equipment

Heater and Thermostat

Tropical fishes and plants are used to water temperatures of about 73° to 79°F (23° to 26°C) and sometimes higher. (Fishes from temperate climates, on the other hand, are used to water temperatures of 50° to 68°F (10° to 20°C).) Therefore, you will need an aquarium heater to heat the water if you want to keep tropical fishes. Generally, fish do not tolerate considerable fluctuations in temperature very well, and the heating system should be thermostatically regulated.

Types of Heaters and Required Capacity

The least expensive heaters are the *electr rod-type heaters,* some of which have no thermostat. *Automatic heaters* come with built-in thermostats. You can also buy thermostats separately, and you can add several more heaters. This may be to your advantage if you have several tanks of equal size and would like to keep them all at the same temperature.

Since the higher capacity rod-type heaters can get very warm when operating, you need to ensure that they do not touch any of the aquarium panels and panes. (Always remember to unplug them before removing them from the water.) They adhere to the aquarium by means of suction cups so that they are in contact with water on all sides. A heater is most effective when mounted vertically in a tank.

In a room with a temperature of 68° to 73°F (20° to 23°C) a heating capacity of 0.3 to 0.5 watt per quart (liter) of water is sufficient because the aquarium has to be heated only a few degrees above room temperature. For an unheated room you will need a stronger heater—one with a capacity of 1 watt per quart (liter) of water.

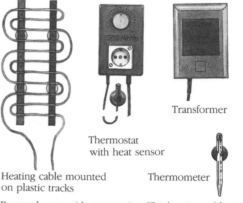

Thermostat with heat sensor

Transformer

Thermometer

Heating cable mounted on plastic tracks

Bottom heater with accessories. The heating cable is either placed on the tank floor or incorporated into the bottom gravel.

Lighting also adds heat to the aquarium, especially when you use a cover with built-in light. In this case, remember to check the temperature daily; it may be necessary to turn off the light on especially hot summer days. The fish will not be too cold if the recommended wattage is followed.

A less powerful heater is cheaper to buy and to operate and also has another advantage. Most thermostats come with a heat sensor with a bimetal contact. A high-capacity heater turns on and off constantly, and the contact soon gets worn. It starts to stick, and at some point it will not open at all. In a matter of hours a strong heater can raise the water temperature to 140°F (60°C) or higher, and you will lose all your fish. A small heater is easier on a thermostat and heats the tank more slowly. If the thermostat fails to operate properly, you have time to save the fish before the water becomes intolerably hot.

Aquarium Equipment

If you do not like cables and rods to mar the view of your fish and the appearance of your aquarium, you may buy an *outside filter with a built-in heater.*

The heaters described above heat only the water in the tank. All aquarium plants, however, like to have "warm feet," and nurseries specializing in water plants recommend keeping the bottom temperature about 1 to 2 degrees above the water temperature. *To heat the bottom,* arrange a waterproof heating cable (it must be approved for this use!) on the bottom of the tank in S-curves. Mount it on plastic tracks or feet so it does not touch the glass and cannot be pressed into the bottom gravel. Alternatively, you can heat the bottom with a heating pad placed directly underneath the aquarium when it is set up, and separated from the supporting surface with an appropriate insulating material. If a heating pad is used, make sure that the bottom gravel is quite coarse (about 3 mm in diameter), because fine sand at the bottom will not conduct heat quickly enough. In that case heat may be trapped and the tank bottom damaged. Glass damage also occurs when a heating pad is too strong or improperly installed.

Since warm water rises to the top, fresh water will flow continuously through the bottom material if a bottom heater is used. This prevents organic matter from rotting on the bottom, brings nutrients to plant roots, and causes the bottom gravel to act as an additional filter. The quality of the water is significantly improved, and the entire aquarium climate becomes more stable. If you use a bottom heater, clean the bottom gravel every year or two because all filters tend to get dirty and become plugged up sooner or later.

A heating pad or heating cable may be sufficient to heat the aquarium without the need for another heater. The bottom heater, however, should not be too powerful. One watt per 10 quarts (liters) of water is enough to circulate the entire volume of water contained in the tank through the bottom gravel once or twice daily. Any current warmer and more powerful will damage the roots of the water plants. A dual-circuit thermostat that regulates the bottom heater and can also turn on the aquarium heater on cold days is recommended. The thermostat for the bottom heater is attached to the outside of the tank; only the heat sensor is attached inside. The heat sensor may also be mounted on the outside of the aquarium glass panel with silicone rubber.

Safety and Other Considerations

Heaters and thermostats are electrical appliances that function under water. The combination of electricity and water is not without its dangers, and these aquarium appliances must be UL-approved for safety. It is still possible, however, to get an electric shock if, for example, a heater in the tank is broken and you happen to reach into the aquarium. Usually the fish do not get hurt. Electrical accidents with an aquarium occur only rarely, but they are unpleasant and you should try your best to prevent them.

The safest type of heating equipment is the heating pad, which rests outside and underneath the tank and has nothing electrical that needs to be submerged in the water. Also safe is the cable-type bottom-heating system because it operates with low currents. A transformer is part of the

Aquarium Equipment

equipment, and heater and thermostat are usually mounted upright so that the top can be above the water surface. Buy only equipment that is waterproof and UL-approved for use in water. Check for commercially available electronic safety devices that eliminate all risks. Installed between the outlet and the safety unit, they shut off the current if there is any malfunction. These units have four plugs, so that you can connect four aquarium heaters or all the electrical equipment of the aquarium. An aquarium should not be grounded.

You may want to keep an additional rod-type or automatic heater on hand in case the heater in the tank malfunctions or ceases to operate. This is particularly important if you keep the tank in an un-heated room. You also need an accurate thermometer that can be mounted on the front glass panel of the tank, perhaps with a suction cup, close to the bottom gravel. Use only an approved thermometer that gives accurate readings.

Optimal Lighting

Duration, Intensity, and Color
For fish and plants artificial lighting is more desirable than natural daylight, over which you have no control. Tropical fishes and plants do not do well in temperate latitudes, where day length changes markedly during the course of a year. Near the equator a day is always 12 hours long. A tropical aquarium should therefore receive evenly controlled lighting 12 to 14 hours daily. Only then will a tropical day be approximated, permitting the fish to live by their own internal clocks. Light is

the primary timekeeper for all animals and plants. To avoid fluctuations in the length of lighting time you can buy a timer that turns the light on and off automatically.

Besides the proper duration, the proper intensity of light is important for plants and fish. For healthy growth tropical plants require approximately the same amount of light as is provided in their native habitats, to which they are adapted. Fish are less demanding and generally need less light. Fortunately, if there is too much light, fish have the option of seeking out darker places among plants and decorative objects. Floating plants tend to soften light.

Correct aquarium lighting: The fish, orienting itself by gravity and by the light entering from above, is properly positioned on a vertical axis.

Even today many aquariums do not have sufficient lighting. Water absorbs light; brown, peat-filtered water absorbs an especially large amount. The ideal amount of light for aquarium lamps is 0.4 to 0.7 watt per quart (liter) of water. An aquarium measuring 36 × 18 × 18 inches (91 × 46 × 46 cm) and holding 50 gallons (190 liters) of water should have a lamp of about 80 to 140 watts. A simple rule of thumb is to use 1 watt per 2 quarts (liters) of water; for example, a 50-gallon (200-

liter) tank needs a 100 watt lamp. Unfortunately, green algae thrive under such conditions. For this reason be sure to include some algae-eating fish when you first set up your aquarium, such as the Siamese Flying Fox *(Epalzeorhynchus siamensis),* some types of bristle-mouth *(Ancistrus* sp.), and Chinese Algae-Eaters *(Gyrinocheilus aymonieri).* In a tank with hard water, the Sphenops Molly *(Poecilia Sphenops)* and the Yucatan Sailfin Molly *(P. velifera)* will be useful.

Even when less than optimal light is present, clean water will enhance plant growth. The high amount of nitrate in dirty water increases the light requirements of plants. The plants will no longer continue to grow, even under optimal lighting conditions.

The closer the color of the aquarium light is to that of sunlight, the more "natural" fish and plants will appear. But in nature also, the color of light varies. Morning and evening sunlight contains a lot of red and appears "warm." Light in the middle of the day contains much blue and appears "cold." Red light encourages vertical growth in plants; blue light furthers strong, compact growth. Aquarium lighting, therefore, must supply the correct balance of red and blue.

Types of Aquarium Lights

Nowadays incandescent bulbs need not be used for aquarium lighting, even though a variety of sizes and colors is available. These bulbs are not suitable for the needs of plants, although their light spectrum feels comfortable to the human eye. Also, they give off too much heat for the amount of light emitted. If you light your aquarium with incandescent bulbs, the tank will get too hot, it will be unnecessarily expensive to operate, and plants will not thrive in the long run.

Incorrect aquarium lighting: If the light enters from the side, the fish gets two different signals for "up," causing it to swim at an angle.

Fluorescent lighting is more energy efficient than incandescent bulbs, and it is possible to combine several types of tubes with variously colored light to achieve a light mixture that suits the needs of the plants. There are white fluorescent lights that approximate normal daylight, "warm-tone" lights that contain a lot of red, and "cold-tone" lights with much blue. An aquarium should have a combination of one warm-tone and one cold-tone fluorescent tube or one warm-tone and one daylight fluorescent tube. Violet grow lights encourage plant growth, but remember they also promote blue-green algae growth if they are turned on when the tank is first set up. You should wait about 3 to 6 months, until plants are well established, before adding these fluorescent grow lights. Keep in mind also that grow lights tend to change the color of the fish; red fish in particular will no longer look natural.

Aquarium Equipment

Fluorescent lights lose their efficiency slowly but steadily. If they are used about 14 hours daily, they lose half of their power after about 6 months. Replace them at least once a year; if you are especially concerned about healthy plant growth, install new ones every 6 months, especially if violet grow lights are used. Plants can be damaged and will usually die if you wait too long before changing these lights.

Aquarium hoods with built-in fluorescent fixtures are available for the standard bulb types—16, 18, 24, and 36 inches (40, 46, 61, and 91 cm). Usually, aquarium lights have one or two tubes, sometimes three or more. If a 36-inch (91-cm)-long aquarium is equipped with only two 36-inch tubes at 30 watts each, plants do not get adequate light. A 50-gallon (190-liter) tank requires 80 to 140 watts, which means at least three tubes. In fact, four tubes would be more appropriate for healthy plant growth.

For your first aquarium, two or three fluorescent tubes will be sufficient. If you start out with hardy, undemanding plants such as *Sagittaria,* the less delicate *Hygrophila* types, or shade-tolerant *Cryptocoryne affinis* plants, you are on your way to a lovely underwater garden. These plants are so hardy that they can withstand a beginner's mistakes, and will grow even with low light. If you should later decide to buy and breed some of the herbivorous characins, the large cichlids, or fish living in brackish waters, you will not need more light because the plants will soon disappear. There will be adequate light for your fish. If, on the other hand, you decide to keep more demanding plants with high light requirements, or if you are toying with the idea of a Dutch plant aquarium, you should consider buying mercury vapor lights.

Mercury vapor lights are not common in the United States. If you can find them, they can be placed on the aquarium or suspended above it. Also, tank covers with these lights built in are available commercially; they contain small openings for heater cables and filter tubing. High-quality products contain no metal parts and are safe to use, so that mishaps such as electric shock cannot occur. Check with your local retailer to learn which products are available.

If lights are placed on top of the tank, the water will be heated. To avoid this additional heat, you can make openings in the light box or in the cover to let some of the heat escape; many covers, as mentioned above, already come with these openings. Also, the heat from the lights will not be a problem if the aquarium heater provides only about 0.4 to 0.7 watt per quart (liter) of water, as recommended.

Hanging lights have the advantage of not heating the water in the tank, and maintenance chores can be done more easily. If the light is on the aquarium cover, you will have difficulty seeing what you are doing because you will have to move the light aside first. If you have the option of hanging the light from the ceiling, therefore, do it. The distance between the light and the cover should be about 4 to 6 inches (10 to 15 cm). When you need to work in the tank, you can raise the light by shortening the cord or chain from which it hangs. Most aquarium lights are equipped with reflectors or are white on the inside to increase light efficiency. You can achieve the same effect by lining the tank cover with foil.

As an aquarium owner you are responsible for the optimal use of your aquarium lighting. The cover should be cleaned weekly. The lighting will not be effective if the cover has a layer of mineral deposits and algae on it. Regularly scheduled changes of water prevent your plants from dying and from becoming excessively dependent on lighting.

Some Special Uses of Various Types of Lights

You can combine fluorescent lighting with other types of lamps if you would like to achieve specific objectives. You may want to add incandescent light bulbs or spotlights to highlight certain areas in your aquarium or a specific plant arrangement, or to show off a particularly interesting back wall.

If you have an aquarium that is low but wide, fluorescent lighting will be most effective. If, however, you own a tall tank more than 20 inches (50 cm) in height and 125 gallons (473 liters) or more in capacity, mercury vapor lights are unsurpassed. Their yield is much higher than that of fluorescent lights, and their operation more economical. The bulbs last much longer than fluorescent tubes. After 2 years of use they will have lost only about 20 percent of their original capacity. This longer life more than makes up for the higher original investment. Mercury vapor lamps do not fit into standard lightbulb sockets, and they need their own shades and a voltage regulator. If, for example, your tank has a water depth of about 20 inches (50 cm), you will need 1.8 watts per ⅜ inch (1 cm) of tank length for optimal lighting; with a depth of 24 inches (60 cm), you will need 2.5 watts per ⅜ inch (1 cm) of tank length.

Mercury vapor lamps reach their full intensity slowly, about 5 minutes after being turned on. The occupants of the aquarium are in for a treat: the effect is almost like a real sunrise! The gradual lighting up of these lamps is much more comfortable for the fish than a sudden change from dark to light, particularly for easily frightened species such as glassfishes, some barbs, and certain types of cichlids. If lights are turned on suddenly, these fishes are liable to be startled enough to jump right out of the tank.

Dutch aquariums should be equipped with mercury vapor lamps if possible. The light of these lamps is so intense that plants will grow out of the tank if no cover is used and plants are not cut back. If there is no tank cover, some marsh plants such as *Cryptocoryne, Aponogeton,* and *Echinodorus* may even flower.

The Filter

A filter is the most important equipment in any aquarium. It removes fish excreta, leftover food, decaying plant material, and other substances from the water and thus improves its quality. The mechanical removal of suspended matter, however, is not the most important task of a filter; biological cleaning and renewed conditioning of the water are much more important for establishing a healthy environment for the plants and fish. Water that has some debris suspended in it and is opaque with blue-green algae is far less harmful than crystal-clear water that is overloaded with waste products. Filters also serve to circulate the water and to produce a more or less powerful current in the aquarium.

The size of the filter should be determined by the number of fish and the plant growth in the aquarium. If the tank has few fish but many plants, the filter can be smaller than if the tank is overcrowded with fish. The larger the filter, the more efficient it will be. It should be capable of circulating at least one-half the water mass—better yet, the entire volume of water in the tank—at least once every hour.

Types of Filters

Small *inside filters,* such as *filters with foam-type material in cartridges and corner filters,* are placed inside a corner of a tank. They are adequate for small aquariums and are also used in breeding and quarantine tanks, where fish are not kept for long periods and the appearance of the aquarium is not important. They are operated with an air pump that sucks air into the filter and forces water through the filter material. A corner filter should not be used in an aquarium containing more than 10 gallons (40 liters) of water. In an aquarium kept mainly for beauty, where appearance is of paramount importance, equipment should be hidden behind plants and decorative objects when possible. The small corner filter will therefore be limited in its function and be less efficient.

Cleaning inside filters is always upsetting for fish; in small tanks the effect is even more traumatic than in large ones. For this reason aquarium hobbyists often avoid cleaning the filter, which becomes clogged as a result. Small filters in particular, which are equipped with less efficient air pumps, will in the end just barely operate. At best, a corner filter may circulate and filter only the water immediately surrounding it and will have absolutely no effect on the remaining water. Filters that use foam materials are easier to clean. An inside filter with a cartridge of activated carbon and/or fiber "floss" is the easiest to operate. The cartridge can be exchanged without lifting the entire filter out of the water.

A *biological filter* should be used as an inside filter for a large aquarium, or you can use an undergravel filter or a combination of both. These filters clean the water biologically. The best biological filter in an aquarium is bottom gravel with water circulating gently through it. Even if a different method of filtering the water is used, a bottom filter can still be added. A bottom filter consists of a grid placed on the bottom of the aquarium and covered with somewhat coarse gravel. This filter pulls water from the bottom down through the gravel by means of an air pump that uses rising air bubbles to circulate the water. A bottom filter is therefore similar to a bottom heater; either one requires that the bottom gravel, which acts as a filter, be replaced or thoroughly cleaned at least once a year, and sometimes even more often.

Another type of inside filter is the *mechanical fast filter,* a water pump with an added filter insert. These filters are primarily designed to remove debris and larger particles from the water. The filter inserts are generally small and contain only a small amount of filter material, often cotton wadding. The filter needs to be cleaned at least once a week, and the filter material washed or replaced, in order not to overload the pump. Mechanical fast filters are quite useful after major renovations or changes in your aquarium because they will clean the water quickly. Water pumps are considerably more efficient than air pumps. They also produce a strong

Aquarium Equipment

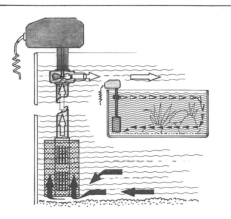

Inside filter with a pump (mechanical fast filter). Water is sucked from below through the filter layer and flows out at the top. This creates a strong water current.

current in the water, which is desirable for many species of fish. Nevertheless, they are no substitute for either a biological filtering system or regular changing of the water.

Outside filters, often called *power filters,* are used if the aquarium hobbyist does not want to have too many gadgets cluttering up the tank—for example, in a decorative aquarium set up in a living room or den. Outside filters should be as large as possible. There are filters with filler inserts for medium-large to large aquariums, 20 to 75 gallons (76 to 283 liters) in capacity, and filters in a variety of sizes (check with your dealer for available products). They are normally equipped with water pumps that force the water through several layers of filter material. It is also possible to place a large filter, working on either a water pump or a large air pump, in an enclosed cabinet next to the aquarium.

Aquariums with built-in filter cabinets are available. Again, consult your dealer before you make your purchase.

For aquariums more than 75 gallons (283 liters) in capacity you may want to choose a filter system that combines filtering and reconditioning the water (biofiltering). Some products, for example, filter water biologically and at the same time permit the use of cartridge-style ion-exchangers and carbon dioxide addition. Other filters, especially suited for large tanks, are even more versatile. They filter water both mechanically and biologically. They even convert nitrate to nitrogen, check the total mineral content, and transfer untreated or prefertilized water from a reserve container into the main tank as needed. These uncommon and very costly items are suitable for the serious aquarium hobbyist.

The high-capacity water-pump filters are particularly important for an aquarium with only a few plants or none at all. They are essential for fish living in densely populated aquariums.

Filter Materials

Whether a filter works at all, and if so how well it works, depends not only on the type of pump but also on the type of filter material used. All filter materials filter large dirt particles from the water mechanically. Coarse filter material removes only the large particles; more densely packed material removes both the large and the smaller particles suspended in water. Frequently bacteria settle on the surface of the filter material and break down organic substances in the water. Some filter media alter the water chemically.

Aquarium Equipment

A mechanical filtering system frequently uses materials such as a kind of wadding, foam, and small clay tubes. Wadding has the advantage that it is easily cleaned.

Activated carbon also acts as a mechanical filter to draw toxic substances from the aquarium water. A carbon filter should be used when medication has to be removed from the water, or after a large fish or several snails have died and too many protein substances may be present in the water. It is also needed when the water becomes cloudy as a result of excess feeding. Chlorine and other harmful chemical substances can be removed from tap water with the help of activated carbon. It is much simpler, however, to condition the water with the numerous special products commercially available for that purpose; consult your dealer. Also, bear in mind that the substances taken up by activated carbon soon break down further the filter, and any of the previously filtered substances may be released again as time goes by. Under the conditions described above, therefore, activated carbon should be used only for about 3 to 4 days; then it must be removed. Nevertheless, every aquarium hobbyist should always have a spare packet of activated carbon on hand for emergencies.

Nitrosomonas and *Nitrobacter* bacteria (see Nitrogen Compounds, page 23) tend to grow on the surface of filter material; they break down nitrogen-bound waste products of the aquarium occupants into comparatively nontoxic nitrate. This is removed by a change of water, or a filter turns it into gaseous nitrogen. The larger the surface of the filter material—that is, the less coarse the material is—the more bacteria will grow on it. You can choose from a variety of products on the market (ask your dealer), or use, for example, fine clay tubes or foam, if a biological filter is needed. Manufacturers also offer a specific filter mass with an extra-large surface for establishing bacteria. The richer the water is in oxygen, the more effective filter bacteria are. Therefore, the water in a filter should be as oxygen-rich as possible.

An ion-exchanger and peat constitute a filter mass that changes water as far as its chemical composition is concerned. Ion-exchanger resins are available that can be used inside the regular filter. For a short period of time they can maintain the quality of soft tropical water. Peat also can be somewhat effective as an ion-exchanger and can soften water. Filtering with peat prevents the growth of algae, kills bacteria and fungi, and encourages greater resistance against diseases that attack the skin of fish. Peat also contains hormone-like substances beneficial to the reproductive function of fish and to plant growth as well. If you buy peat for filter use only at your aquarium store, where it is available in small fabric bags, you can be reasonably assured that the product will be reliable and effective.

Peat may color the water either yellow or brown. Some types of peat color the water more than other types. The color of the water, however, is no indication of how efficient your peat filter is.

Egg layers.
Above left: Steel-blue Aphyosemion *(Aphyosemion gardneri)*; above right: Chevalier's Epiplatys *(Epiplatys chevalieri)*; middle left: Red-chinned Panchax *(Epiplatys chaperi)*; middle right: Firemouth Pondrax *(E. dageti monroviae)*; below left: *Nothobranchius rachovi*; below right: Argentine Pearlfish *(Cynolebias nigripinnis)*.

Aquarium Equipment

Filter Maintenance

How often a filter should be cleaned depends on its size, the quality of the water, the number and size of the fish, and the kind of food they receive. Filter wadding and all other materials used for mechanical filtering have to be cleaned or replaced as soon as the filter insert becomes dirty. A clogged filter does not necessarily impede the water flow because the filter mass normally still has a few openings for water to flow through; the problem is that the water is circulating through the filter without being cleaned. Filter wadding should be cleaned once a week; carbon and peat should be replaced after 3 to 4 weeks. Carbon and peat cannot be cleaned or used again.

Any material used for a biological filter should stay in the filter as long as possible. A new biological filter takes 3 to 4 months before it works well and reaches peak efficiency. A biological filter may remain for more than a year in an aquarium that has been well planted and in which the fish have been carefully fed. On the other hand, you will probably have to clean the filter after about 3 or 4 months if your aquarium is heavily populated and your fish are overfed. Bacteria are destroyed by hot water, so you must clean the filter with cold or lukewarm water only. If you have reusable filter material, rinse it until no traces of debris are left.

If the pump breaks down, causing the water flow through the filter to be interrupted or the filter to run on "empty," the filter must be cleaned thoroughly.

Advice to the Beginner: Buy the aquarium and the filter at the same time. Informed pet-store personnel can advise you as to the proper kind and size of filter, and type of filter material, for your aquarium and your fish, and will tell you how to take care of the filter. Do not skimp on the filter—it is your aquarium's life-support system.

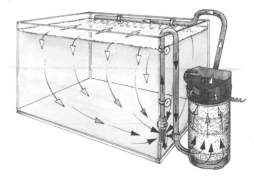

Outside filter with pump. The pump is located in the lid of the filter unit. It forces the water from the bottom up through the filter material and out through a pipe that leads back into the tank.

Water Circulation and Aeration

Filters not only clean the water, they also circulate it. An aquarium needs water movement because all aquarium fish originally lived in water that was in more or less constant motion. Even stagnant water is acted on by wind, so that it is never as still as the water in an aquarium would be without a filter. In a tank with no filter or aeration, a layer of bacteria forms at the

Live bearers.
Above left: Swordtail *(Xiphophorus helleri)*; above right: Guppy *(Poecilia reticulata)*; middle left: Sunset Platy *(X. variatus)*; middle right: Black Molly *(P. sphenops)*; below left: Giant Sailfin Molly *(P. velifera)*; below right: Platy *(X. maculatus)*.

water surface, a kind of "skin" that, in combination with a layer of dust, forms an almost airtight barrier and impedes the essential exchanges between air and surface water. (If this type of "skin" appears in spite of aeration, use blotting paper to remove it.) Water gives up carbon dioxide and takes up oxygen at the surface. The water surface therefore needs to be in constant motion so that exchange of gases can take place.

The numbers of fish and of plants in an aquarium determine how much water circulation is required and whether additional aeration is needed. The breakdown of nitrogen requires a great deal of oxygen and produces carbon dioxide. Therefore, the water that comes out of the filter is poor in oxygen and rich in CO_2. Plants need CO_2 as fertilizer, but fish suffocate in water saturated with this gas. Whereas fish need oxygen in order to breathe, plants produce it as a by-product while they are in sunshine. If an aquarium is stocked with healthy plants and few fish, the plants will take up all available CO_2. The water in such a tank needs only gentle movement, with no additional aeration, so that CO_2 does not escape.

Unfortunately, the average aquarium has many fish and relatively few plants. In many tanks the fish are crowded together with fish just a few neglected, algae-covered plants. If you cannot reduce the number of fish, only powerful circulation of the water and perhaps additional aeration can assure the well-being of your fish. In particular, aquariums filled with herbivorous fishes such as cichlids and some types of characins, as well as tanks with fishes that live in brackish water, need strong aeration.

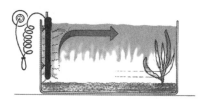

Aquarium with poor water circulation. Warm water moves up only while the heater is on. There is always a layer of cold water just above the floor. Circulation is so slow that hot and cold water do not mix.

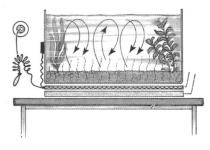

Aquarium with good water circulation. Bottom heating causes freshly warmed water to rise constantly, and cold and warm water mix quickly.

As a general rule sufficient aeration can be provided by installing a filter in such a way that the outlets are exactly at the water surface. Then the water is kept in circular motion without bubbling up too much and letting carbon dioxide escape before it can benefit the plants. If excess CO_2 is a problem, the filtered water should be returned to the tank from above the water surface. Water-pump filters also have jets that dissipate the stream of water and thus promote the exchange of gases.

If the filter is run by an air pump and is not strong enough, the tank needs additional aeration. An airstone is then mounted on the side of the tank opposite the filter and is driven by the air pump. An airstone creates many small air bubbles, with more surface area than a few large bubbles. The exchange of gases is increased because water can absorb oxygen only when it is in direct contact with the air. The smaller the bubbles from the airstone, the more oxygen is released into the water.

An aquarium that contains many fish and few or no plants needs strong aeration, and should not be covered tightly because carbon dioxide has to be able to escape. On the other hand, a Dutch aquarium needs a tight cover to keep the CO_2 in the tank for the plants.

The water current that a filter and an airstone create in a tank is important for fish and plants alike. In particular, fishes that have adapted to fast-moving water in their native habits do best when they swim against the current produced by the filter. If the tank is large enough, you should provide them with such a current by means of a water pump. Mount the filter to the tank is such a way that the entire aquarium is evenly aerated, the water is well circulated, and the formation of warmer and cooler areas within the tank is avoided. By sprinkling a little debris on the water, you can tell how the water moves in your aquarium and what improvements, if any, are needed.

Useful Accessories

A great variety of accessories and decorative items is available in specialty stores. Many of them are unnecessary, but others are essential.

You need *attachments for your filter and aeration systems.* If the filter and airstone are driven by an air pump, you will need a few yards of narrow plastic tubing that enables the air to flow from the pump to the filter and to the airstone. Valves and clamps are necessary to regulate the air flow. These items should be made of plastic or stainless-steel-covered metal. Do not use plain brass clamps, which may form verdigris quickly because of the damp air and will then be extremely toxic to the fish.

Because you will want to catch a fish from time to time, you will need a fairly large *fish net.* If you buy a small net, you will have to pursue the fish more actively, thereby upsetting all the fish and perhaps

Aquarium for beginners. The tank is about 35 inches (80 cm) long and is equipped with light tubes, a thermostatic heater, and a small biological filter (1 heater, 2 pump, 3 filter). The tank is stocked with live bearers and catfish.

Aquarium Equipment

injuring the plants. Catching small fish with a *glass trap* is even easier on the fish; fish traveling in schools, especially, can be caught more easily in this way. With their lateral-line sense organs the fish feel something approaching, but they cannot tell exactly what it is. If you like, you can use a net to drive the fish into the glass trap.

Plant tongs or *tweezers* are used to thin out established plants and to plant new ones. You can also use them to remove rocks, snails, and dead fish from the aquarium.

To siphon off debris and to change the water, you need a *hose* about 5 feet (1.5 meters) long and ½ to ¾ inch (1 to 2 cm) in interior diameter. You will also need at least two *buckets,* which cannot be used for household cleaning, since remnants of soap and cleaning detergents are extremely toxic to fish. Using a waterproof marking pen, write "Aquarium" on the buckets in large letters, and make it clear to all family members that the buckets are not to be used for any other purpose. Watering cans or buckets with spouts are better than plain ones because they are easier to pour from.

To clean the front panel of the tank, you need a *window wiper* with a felt, sponge, or razor edge but without brass parts. A wiper with a sponge on one side and a scrubbing pad on the other is generally safe and satisfactory. The usual green-algae layer can be wiped off with the sponge side, and the tougher algae and calcium deposits can be scrubbed away with the rough side. There are also window wipers with magnets. One magnet is placed with its cleaning surface on the inside of the tank's front panel; the other is moved over the glass on the outside, so as to pull along the inside magnet, which does the cleaning.

Be careful not to stir up sand or gravel from the bottom when cleaning, or you will scratch the glass. You can make deep scratches in the glass if you do not use a window wiper with a razor edge carefully. Keep in mind that algae love to grow in these scratches, which you will not be able to clean or remove; at the very least, they will be an eyesore if you want to photograph your fish.

Another essential item is a *timer* to turn the light on and off at the same time every day. Anyone who is serious about keeping fish also needs kits to measure pH, hardness, ammonia, and nitrite since it is imperative to be aware of the chemical processes going on in the water. It may also be possible to obtain electronic control panels that keep track of the water level, hardness, conductivity, pH, amount of oxygen, and other factors; they turn the light on and off and sometimes even control an automatic feeding dispenser. Such sophisticated and expensive equipment, however, is designed for serious breeders, special aquatic institutes and facilities, and aquarium-store owners.

Setting Up the Aquarium

Once your aquarium is placed where you want it, on a level surface, you can begin to equip and decorate it. First, rinse the tank again with clean water to remove any traces of detergents or other potentially harmful substances. Then, before filling the tank with water, install the necessary equipment. Now use your creative imagination to decorate your aquarium and to provide a beautiful, livable environment for your fish.

The Back Wall

It is not essential to decorate the back wall for the fish, but looking through the tank at a plain wall of a room seems to take away some of the magic from the green underwater world of an aquarium. If you paint the back wall black or gray, using waterproof color on the outside, the aquarium appears to gain depth and the fish seem to feel safer. You can also create a backdrop by gluing reeds, grasses, bark, and similar decorative materials on a piece of cardboard or wood and then mounting it behind the aquarium. Decorative back walls are also available commercially. Unfortunately, there is a disadvantage to

Back wall made from polyester material. Decorative items are placed on a framed board and then covered with liquid polyester resin.

attaching a decorative backdrop to the outside of the tank: the inside back wall gradually gets covered by algae, and the decorations become less and less visible unless you clean the glass frequently. That is not desirable, however, because cleaning upsets the fish.

Back walls mounted on the inside of the tank must be nontoxic and constructed so that none of the fish can get caught in or behind any surface. A tank holding less than 50 gallons (190 liters) is better off without an expensive back wall decoration, which tends to take up too much room. For a large aquarium, however, you can take advantage of such a backdrop. A rough, rugged wall offers safety for young fish and provides timid fish with protection from larger, more aggressive species because protrusions and hollows provide hiding places. Rough structures, more than plain glass walls, also offer additional surface areas where algae can thrive, and almost all fish consider algae a welcome additional food. A further advantage is that such a backdrop can supply a practical hiding place for heating cables and hoses or tubing.

You can build a back wall yourself. Use only products such as polyurethane or polyester resin that are safe for fish and plants. For a polyester wall you will need a sheet panel covered with liquid plastic and finished with a wooden frame. On the panel arrange rocks, sand, and other materials of your choice to form a natural-looking backdrop, resembling, for example, a river bank. Pour epoxy between and over these materials to make everything stick together well. To give individual parts, or the entire backdrop, an even structure and color, you can pour sand over everything. Finally, coat the entire back wall with one layer of epoxy. It will harden in about an hour, and the wooden frame can then be removed. Allow the backdrop to air out for about 10 days, and then soak it thoroughly for 1 week. You can then mount it in your aquarium. This type of back wall is quite heavy because of the materials used.

You can also buy back walls made of nontoxic polyurethane that are quite light. They have to be glued or clamped to the tank until they have soaked up enough water and will not float around. These back walls are available in sheets of varied thickness; the best choice is sheets about 2½ to 3 inches (6 to 8 cm) thick. You create your own surface by digging out caves and canyons and building up protrusions to construct hiding places for your fish. Once you are satisfied with your work, continue to pluck at the entire surface until it resembles porous lava. (Depending on the size of the back wall, you may need gloves for this job because polyurethane can be rough on your hands.) Attach the finished product to the frame of the tank with silicone caulk, and keep it in place with rocks. After 1 to 2 weeks, when it has soaked up sufficient water, it will stay in place without support. Alternatively, you can use silicone caulk to glue the wall to the glass in the back. (Be sure that the silicone caulk is the type that is suitable for aquariums, and that sufficient time is allowed for the silicone to cure.) Polyurethane walls can be covered with *Microsorium pteropus, Vesicularia dubyana,* or other plants that do not have to root in the bottom gravel. If you and the fish leave them alone, in time these plants will cover the entire back wall.

Back wall made from polyurethane. Digging out pieces of the polyurethane will create caves and canyons that your fish can use as hiding places.

Bottom Material and Rocks

Most tropical fish and plants originally lived in waters quite poor in calcium; in other words, they have adapted to very soft water. Bottom material and rocks in a tropical aquarium therefore should contain no calcium because you want to avoid unnecessarily hard water for the occupants. On the other hand, a few rocks containing some calcium are harmless in tanks with fish used to living in brackish water, in tanks with cichlids from East African lakes, and in tanks for European and North American fishes. They live in temperate climates and have adapted to medium-hard and hard water.

It is quite easy to test bottom material or rocks for calcium. Place a few drops of dilute hydrochloric acid on the substance to be tested: if you see bubbles forming, the material contains calcium and should not be used.

The Correct Bottom Material
The bottom material is more important for plants than for fish. Plants will root in it and get their nutrients from it. They will do well only when the bottom material is

loose and well aerated, and that means it cannot be too fine. It must also be deep enough, so buy enough for 2- to 2½-inch (5- to 6-cm) layer. One of the more common bottom materials is quartz gravel, which can be bought in various grades of coarseness. Plants prefer sand 1 to 2 millimeters in diameter. Finer sand prevents good water circulation; on the other hand, coarser gravel allows debris to settle to the bottom, where it is difficult to siphon off. Quartz gravel has been heat-treated and no longer contains any nutrients. That is not important, however, because you will fertilize your plants with bottom fertilizer or fertilizer tablets.

If you have a small tank, you can buy the gravel at a pet store. If you need 100 pounds or more, it will be cheaper to buy at a builder's supply outlet. Be sure to ask for quartz gravel because sand or gravel from rivers, for example, may contain calcium. The more expensive prewashed gravel will save a lot of time and effort. All gravel has to be washed thoroughly before it can be used in an aquarium. If at all possible, wash the gravel outdoors. If you must wash it indoors, be especially careful when you pour out the water because sand or gravel can easily clog your drains. Fill a 2½-gallon (10-liter) bucket up to about one-fifth or one-fourth with gravel, add water, and stir vigorously (you may want to wear gloves or use a stick). As soon as the gravel has settled, pour out the water. Repeat this rinsing process until the water is clear or at least almost clear. Prewashed gravel must be rinsed three to five times; unwashed gravel, at least twice as many times.

Unfortunately, fine quart gravel is usually light gray in color and strongly reflects the light that enters the tank from above, so that the tank will be quite bright unless it is shaded by floating plants. North American sunfishes and some other species of fish are not bothered by this bright light, but most tropical fishes avoid it. Many of these species live in black-water regions and are used to dim light.

Polyurethane back wall

Glass strips   Polyvinyl chloride (PVC) and plastic strips

A terraced tank floor. By gluing glass strips and/or polyvinyl chloride and plastic strips to the bottom of the tank to form terraces, and then covering them with rocks and gravel, you can create scenic visual effects.

Coarser quartz gravel, 3 to 5 millimeters in diameter, is available in various shades of brown, and its color absorbs at least some of the light. There is also a very attractive, darker bottom material, a type of dark red-brown lava rock, but this kind of gravel is quite abrasive and therefore not suitable for bottom dwellers and other fishes that like to burrow and poke around in the bottom. This is also true of the darker kind of basalt, which is not suitable for such fishes because of its sharp edges. If you keep armored-plated corydoras and barbs and would like soft bottom material to accommodate their burrowing habits, you can place fine sand or boiled peat in certain areas of your tank. Unfortunately, peat tends to make the water quite murky if fish agitate it.

If you have bought a bottom filter or a heating cable, install it before or while you introduce the bottom material. This is also the time to add the initial fertilizer to the bottom gravel for healthy plant growth (see Fertilizing the Bottom Material, page 60).

The bottom material should be arranged so that it is lower in the front than in the back of the tank. This has a scenic effect and is beneficial for larger plants, which are arranged toward the back of the tank and provided with more rooting material than is available for the smaller plants in the foreground. Loosely poured sand or gravel will be quickly leveled by the fish, and the bottom of the aquarium, especially if the tank is large, will look flat and plain. One solution is to construct the bottom in the shape of terraces, but a terraced effect achieved with rocks and wood will not last. The whole thing will eventually level out again because of water movement and fish activity. Instead, you can glue glass strips to the bottom of the tank and then cover them with rocks and gravel, or you can try strips of hard polyvinyl chloride (PVC) and plastic, which are pliable when heated, so that you can build curved steps for the bottom material. Polyurethane strips can also look natural when shaped into cliffs and slopes. At specialty stores you can also buy plastic building blocks for a terraced effect in your aquarium.

Caution: Any material such as silicone, polyurethane, or heat-treated PVC must be allowed sufficient curing time. It should also soak through several water changes before fish are introduced.

Suitable Rocks

Rocks not only enhance the appearance of an aquarium but also play a very important part in the lives of the fish. They divide the tank into several areas, which are used by fishes that need to mark their own specific territories. The rocks serve to mark the borderlines. Also, fish that are being chased by more aggressive species have a place to hide. Cave dwellers, for example, find safety in hollows under or between rocks, and fishes with protective breeding habits have a place to spawn and raise their fry. Rocks also provide a good surface for algae and other small organisms to settle on, and several aquarium plants will grow on rocks. In this case, porous rocks like lava are more suitable than smooth rocks.

The hardest and most durable of all rocks are the granites, syenites, diorite, gabbro, and the like. These stones are totally devoid of calcium salts, so that you can use them in any freshwater aquarium. Some stones in this group, however, may yield some acidity.

Volcanic basalt rock, diabase, and melaphyrous rocks are of denser consistency than are lava stone and pumice. All of the volcanic rocks are quite suitable for any aquarium; however, pumice is impractical because it is so porous and light that it floats in water.

Sand, gravel, mud, and other organic materials have been combined and hardened by geological pressure and chemical reactions. Sand deposits, for example, turned into sandstone, while other sediments, such as limestone, developed through conglomeration of other minerals—for example, the debris of shells and ocean-derived organisms. These latter formations contain mainly calcium salt, and therefore are not suitable for an aquarium. It is recommended that you test sedimentary rocks for calcium content, since sandstone, as well as other conglomeration-type stones, may well contain this unwanted mineral. You can test for calcium salts by using dilute hydrochloric acid (HCl).

Marble is derived from calcium deposits, making it unsuitable for aquariums. Other metamorphous stones may be used in freshwater tanks; however, it is advisable to test them first with HCl.

If you use many different types of stones, you risk achieving an unnatural look. Remember that a pond, a lake, or a river usually has only one kind of stone or rock formation. It is better to limit yourself to one or two types of stones, which you can choose in various sizes and combinations of structures. One kind of stone is usually sufficient for a small tank, and two for a larger tank.

All rocks must be washed and scrubbed thoroughly before they are put into the aquarium. If they crumble and break easily or contain obvious traces of metal, do not use them. The optimum size and number of rocks in the tank are determined by the needs of the fish. Characins, for example, and fish that travel in schools need a large swimming area, and a few rocks as background are generally sufficient. Catfishes and other cave dwellers need "a roof over

Tank floor

Tank floor

Catfish in a cave. Stone formations must rest directly on the floor of the tank to prevent fish from digging underneath and collapsing the structure.

their head." You can build a cave with small rocks covered by a larger rock like a roof (see drawing, page 47), making the structure look casual and natural. To keep the aggressive cichlids, you will have to build larger rock formations that are as high as one-half the height of the tank or may even reach the water surface. Arrange several smaller rocks in the front of the tank to create some visual territorial areas. Because cichlids tend to burrow frequently during spawning, the lowest rock of a stone structure must rest directly on the floor of the tank so that the fish cannot burrow underneath and topple the entire formation. This not only would injure or kill the fish but also could break one of the glass panels.

Of course, all structures must be safe and stable. Reddish brown, rough, porous lava is one of the best kind of stone to use for such structures. Though rarely seen in nature, it is available in pet stores. Several pieces of lava will stick together much better than smooth stones, and you will find it easier to build even large structures with lava rock. Because of its porosity it is quite light and can be disassembled and removed quickly, if necessary—for example, if you need to rescue a fish attacked by a more aggressive one, or a mouth-brooding female or small fry. It is very difficult indeed to catch a cichlid in a well-decorated aquarium. Female cochlids and lower ranking fish, especially, have become experts at playing hide-and-go-seek and avoiding capture. You can easily catch the "big boss," however, in an aquarium full of cichlids. Unlike the other fish, he does not have to hide and you can quickly find him, even between large rock structures. When lava rock is removed from the tank, in a rescue mission or for another reason, it should be placed in a bucket or a tub, since it is porous and soaked with water, which will surely drain out.

You can also place either half or whole flower pots in the bottom material, especially if you keep cave breeders and bottom dwellers. You may not like how the pots look, but many fish use them for spawning. New pots must be soaked for 1 day in water and peat. (Use about 10 quarts of water and two handfuls of peat.) The humic acid from the peat binds aluminum that may have been introduced when the pots were manufactured. Old clay pots need not be soaked.

Wood and Other Decorative Materials

At the pet store you can sometimes buy wood that has lain airtight in acid soil for so many years that there is nothing left

that can rot. This wood must be cleaned thoroughly and then boiled until it becomes saturated with water and will no longer float to the surface. If large pieces of wood do not fit into your cooking pots, put the wood in the bathtub and run water over it; the longer the time and the hotter the water, the better. Once placed in your aquarium, the wood may have to be weighted down for a few weeks or months, until it no longer floats to the surface. Sometimes a large piece of wood may never become saturated with water.

Spawning bitterlings next to a clam shell. Shells are essential in the tank when breeding bitterlings.

There are several techniques for mounting such pieces of wood in an aquarium. You can glue them to the tank walls or incorporate them in an artificial back wall. They must be fastened securely lest they float around. Fill in all spaces between wood and back wall (check for appropriate products with your retailer) to prevent the buildup of "dead areas" where water will remain stagnant and become foul. If you use small pieces of driftwood and tree trunks to decorate the bottom of the tank, you can prevent floating by tying them with nylon cord to a glass panel and placing it under the gravel. If the wood still tends to float, weight down the glass panel with some rocks and hide these in the gravel also. Catfishes and other species needing hiding places especially prefer driftwood roots. Some algae-eating catfishes (*Plecostomus* and *Loricaria*) spend most of their time under such roots during the day. Sometimes they will not let go of the wood even when you remove it from the tank. For this reason you need to inspect all wood roots carefully and remove any catfishes before you clean out your tank, lest your fish end up on dry land.

In rare cases such tree roots may release nitrite into the water. When you introduce new wood as decoration in your aquarium, therefore, you should test the water in the tank for the presence of nitrite during the first week. If nitrite is present, immediately remove the roots from the tank.

Cave dwellers also like coconut shells. These must also be boiled thoroughly before use.

As soon as you have decorated your aquarium with bottom gravel, rock formations, and driftwood or other decorative roots, you can begin planting (see page 56). To prevent stems and leaves from drying out, however, first fill your tank up to one-third with water.

Filling the Tank with Water

When filling your aquarium with water, be careful not to stir up the gravel and thereby cloud the water, especially if you have

Catfish

Algae-eating catfish. The suction mouth enables the fish to hold on to surfaces and to rub off algae.

already added the initial fertilizer for your water plants below the top layer of gravel. A good procedure is to place a large plate in the tank and slowly pour water on it with a watering can, bucket, or hose. In a small tank without large rock structures you can spread wrapping paper on the bottom of the tank and remove it as soon as the tank is filled with water. Do not use this method for large aquariums, however, because the paper will remain in the tank too long. If you fill the tank directly from the faucet with a hose, watch out that the hose does not slip out of the tank; weigh it down with the tank cover or a rock. Even when you know that it may take quite a while to fill the tank, keep your mind on the job. This is not the time to read a magazine or make telephone calls; aquariums tend to spill over the minute you forget about them. Only if your tank is located in a basement with a drain floor, can you afford to be temporarily absent-minded.

Aquarium Plants

Some Facts About Aquatic Plants

With the exception of some ferns and moss, aquarium plants are flowering plants with roots, stems, leaves, and blossoms. Unlike all other plants, the leaves of aquatic water plants do not have a special coating that protects them against dehydration. They are therefore able to take up nutrients with their leaves directly from the water. Aquatic plants that live submerged under water use their roots less for food intake and more as an anchor. A good example of a plant that is totally submerged in water all year long is *Egeria densa* (see drawing, page 53). Its leaves are thin, delicate, and feathered to increase the surface area that absorbs the nutrients.

Plants from swamps or from rivers with fluctuations in their water level develop tough, firm underwater leaves during dry periods, when they must get their nourishment through their roots from the bottom soil. When planted in an aquarium, they continue to nourish themselves mostly through the roots, even though always submerged in water, and you have to remember this when you fertilize them (see page 59). Examples of swamp plants are the Amazon Sword Plant *(Echinodorus)* and some types of *Hygrophila* (see drawing, page 53).

Role of Plants in the Aquarium

In order to live, plants must be able to breathe continuously. Like human beings and other animals, they use up oxygen from their environment and give off carbon dioxide. With the help of water and CO_2, the green parts of plants produce the carbohydrates that serve as their building blocks—first they turn them into sugar, which is then converted into starches and cellulose. In this process, oxygen is set free (and made available to the fish in the aquarium). This process, called *photosynthesis,* takes place only when light is present in sufficient intensity and over enough time. At night or with insufficient lighting, plants just breathe; they use up oxygen without producing it, and at this point they start to compete with the fish.

In addition to carrying out photosynthesis under optimal conditions (adequate light, warmth, and fertilizer) and giving off oxygen, plants improve the water quality by absorbing from the water nitrogen-containing substances that may have potentially harmful effects on fish. Healthy plant roots also supply the bottom material with oxygen that helps breakdown wastes into harmless substances. Moreover, plants provide surfaces for algae and bacteria that assist the filter in the removal of waste products. Fish nibble at these colonies growing on the plant leaves and thereby find an additional source for food.

Thus, healthy plant growth helps to create a favorable and stable environment for aquarium fish, even though plants cannot create a genuine biological balance in the artificial conditions within an aquarium. You would be well advised to pay close attention to the needs of your water plants. Choose for the tank only plants that place similar demands on their environment (see descriptions of plants and drawings, pages 52 to 55); and that have adapted to the same water conditions and temperatures as the fishes you want to keep (see descriptions of fish species, pages 114 to 137). Plants such as most

Aquarium Plants

Cryptocoryne species, *Aponogeton,* and *Cabomba* need soft water and should not be planted in the same tank with hard-water plants like *Vallisneria* and *Egeria.*

Growth, Selection, and Distribution of Aquarium Plants

Because of the various shapes and growth habits, different plants can be used for specific purposes in an aquarium:

• Stemmed plants, with small leaves *(Hygrophila, Heteranthera, Rotala, Ludwigia)* arranged in twos or in a spiral shape around the stem, quickly form compact masses that provide perfect refuge for small fry and weaker fishes.

• Plants like *Vallisneria* and *Sagittaria* (arrowhead) can be used to shade part of the aquarium from strong light. Leaves are ribbon-like and rise from the bottom to the water surface. Plants grow well and produce many runners. It is safe to remove algae-covered plant parts or even entire plants from time to time.

• Plants with leaves arranged in a rosette shape, such as *Cryptocoryne,* certain kinds of *Echinodorus,* and *Aponogeton,* are the most beautiful plants for an aquarium and make the most attractive display even when planted singly. If you have a large tank, you can create dense growths with them, which will be used for hiding places and for spawning by large fishes (*Echinodorus* thickets for angelfishes).

• Moss and delicate-stemmed plants such as *Ceratophyllum* and *Myriophyllum* are suitable for spawning.

• Floating plants serve to subdue strong light entering the tank from above.

It is just about impossible to arrange plants in an absolutely perfect, biologically

Water Crowfoot *(Ranunculus aquatilis).* This plant clearly shows the difference between submerged and above-surface leaves. The submerged leaves are delicately branched; the surface leaves are lobed.

balanced fashion in an aquarium. In their original habitats, you would probably find only a very few species of plants in a space the size of your tank. It is probable, however, that you will be satisfied with one kind of plant only if you have an aquarium designed for just one type of fish and you want to keep the decorations as natural as possible.

Perhaps the most attractive appearance will be achieved by growing only a few types of plants, with enough specimens of each to arrange groupings. Add one striking single plant—or several in a large aquarium—that catches the viewer's eye. If a tank has a mix of many single plants, each a different type, it is apt to appear unnatural. Three to five kinds of rooted plants and one variety of floating plant are sufficient for a medium-sized tank of 30 to 50 gallons (115 to 190 liters).

Aquarium Plants

Aponogeton undulatus
Madagascar Sword Plant

Modest care requirements. Height 12 to 15 inches (30–40 cm). Plant alone or in groups; new shoots after 2 to 3 months. Light: bright. Water: 68°–82°F (20°–28°C); pH 6.0–7.5; 5°–15° dH. Propagation: offshoots on the flower stem. Other varieties: soft water, bright to very bright; frequent blooms; seed propagation. Habitat: Southeast Asia.

Cabomba caroliniana
Fanwort

Hardiest plant; for loose arrangements; clean, clear water with CO_2 added. Protect from algae and loose debris. Light: very bright. Water: 72°–82°F (22°–28°C); pH 6.5–7.2; 2°–12°dH. Propagation: plantlets. Other varieties: soft water; bright; iron supplement needed. Habitat: South America and North America.

Ceratopteris thalictroides
Water Sprite

Fast growing; bushy, large; for large tanks. Allow top of root to show above ground when planting. Suitable also as floating plant, as spawning substrate and for protection. Light: bright to very light. Water: 68°–82°F (20°–28°C); pH 6.5–7.5; 3°–15°dH. Propagation: leaf edges grow shoots. Habitat: worldwide in tropical zones.

Cryptocoryne affinis

Hardiest of this species. Height 4 to 12 inches (10–30 cm). Suitable for groups. Leaves are red on the bottom side, green on top. Easily affected by disease. Iron supplement needed. Light: bright to shade. Water: 72°–82°F (22°–28°C); pH: 6.0–7.5; 3–13°dH. Propagation: runners are very productive. Habitat: Malaysia.

Cryptocoryne crispatula

Height 12 to more than 20 inches (30–50 cm). Suitable for loose grouping for large tanks. Leaves are less variegated in low than in bright light. Needs well-fed bottom material and iron supplement. Light: bright to half-shade. Water: 75°–82°F (24°–28°C); pH 6.5–7.2; 2°–12°dH; Propagation: runners. Habitat: Southeast Asia.

Echinodorus bleheri
Amazon Sword Plant

Height up to 23 inches (60 cm). Singly or, in large tanks, in groups. Iron supplement needed. Light: bright or half-shaded. Water: 72°–82°F (22°–28°C); pH 6.5–7.5; 2°–15°dH. Propagation: plantlets will grow at the whorls of the flowering stems. These new shoots divide, eventually, into entire plants. Habitat: tropical South America.

Aquarium Plants

Echinodorus cordifolius
Amazon Sword with Heart-shaped Leaves

More than 15 inches (40 cm) high. Trim floating leaves when they get large. Trim root runners, also. Light: bright. Water: 72°–82°F (22°–28°C); pH 6.5–7.5; 5°–15°dH. Propagation: After blooming, seeds can be used; otherwise, new plant shoots. Habitat: subtropical North America.

Egeria densa

This robust plant grows fast, is great for beginners, cleans the water, produces oxygen, and is most suitable for water with high calcium content. With bright lighting it is good for tropical aquariums. Light: bright. Water: 64°–79°F (18°–26°C); pH 6.5–7.5; 8°–18°dH. Propagation: plantlets. Habitat: Central America and South America.

Eichhornia crassipes
Water Hyacinth

Floating plant. Grows large and extensively. Has blue leaves in open tanks. Cleans water fast; uses O_2 from the air and nitrogen byproducts from the water. Light: bright or very bright. Water: 72°–82°F (22°–28°C); pH 6.0–7.8; 2°–15°dH. Propagation: side runners and branching shoots. Habitat: tropical Americas and world-wide.

Heteranthera zosterifolia

Grows very fast with bright light and good fertilization. Need regular trimming. Forms thickets suitable as background plants. Light: bright or very bright. Water: 72°–82°F (22°–28°C); pH 6.0–7.5; 3°–15°dH. Propagation: plantlets. Habitat: Central America and South America.

Hygrophila corymbosa

Fast growing plant for group arrangements or background. Can also grow singly. Needs replanting frequently. Needs iron supplement, especially for red varieties. Cannot tolerate pH below 6.0. Light: bright. Water: 72°–82°F (22°–28°C); pH 6.5–7.5; 2°–15°dH. Propagation: plantlets. Habitat: Southeast Asia.

Hygrophila difformis
Indian Water Star

Good as group plant in large aquariums. Grows fast with good fertilization. Leaves shed when lighting is insufficient. Leaves are small in cool water. Good for beginners. Light: Very bright. Water: 77°–82°F (25°–28°C); pH 6.5–7.5; 2°–15°dH. Propagation: plantlets. Habitat: Southeast Asia.

Aquarium Plants

Hygrophila polysperma
Indian Water Friend

Hardy, modest, fast-growing. With good fertilization, suitable for beginners. Needs trimming and thinning regularly. Forms thickets. Light: Bright. Water: 64°–86°F (18°–30°C); pH 6.5–7.5; 3°–15°dH. Propagation: plantlets. Habitat: India.

Microsorium pteropus
Java Fern

Amphibian plant. Roots by itself when tied to stones, roots, or background wall. Trim as soon as black spots occur. Light: not too bright. Water: 72°–82°F (22°–28°C); pH 5.5–7.0; 2°–12°dH. Propagation: shoots on leaves and roots. Habitat: Southeast Asia.

Limnophila sessiliflora

Group plant. Needs to be trimmed and replanted and protected from algae and dirt. Needs iron. Light: very bright. Water: 72°–82°F (22°–28°C); pH 6.0–7.5; 3°–15°dH. Propagation: plantlets. Habitat: Southeast Asia.

Myriophyllum aquaticum

Suitable for loosely arranged groups. Protect from algae and debris. Needs replanting. Good as spawning substrate. Light: bright. Water: 72°–86°F (22°–30°C); pH 5.0–7.5; 2°–12°dH. Propagation: plantlets. Habitat: South America.

Ludwigia palustris and Repens (natans)
Needle-Leaf and Green Ludwigia

Variable group plant; red and green varieties. Trimming encourages branching. Iron needed. Suitable for cold water tanks. Light: bright. Water: 63°–82°F (17°–28°C); pH 5.8–7.5; 3°–15°dH. Propagation: Plantlets. Habitat: North America.

Nymphaea lotus
Tiger Lotus

Green, red, or spotted varieties. Singly for large tanks. Has large, floating leaves. Blooms at night. Needs frequent fertilizing. Light: bright or very bright. Water: 72°–82°F (22°–28°C); pH 5.5–7.5; 4°–12°dH. Propagation: seeds, runners. Habitat: Africa, Southeast Asia.

Aquarium Plants

Pistia stratiotes
Water Lettuce

Floating plant. Does not tolerate condensation water; therefore, place tank cover at an angle. Roots serve as spawning substrate and as hiding places. Light: bright or very bright. Water: 72–79°F (22°–26°C); pH 6.5–7.2; 5°–15°dH. Propagation: Runners, prolific. Habitat: worldwide, tropics, and subtropics.

Sagittaria subulata

Produces large, bright green leaves (may become reddish in strong light). Very useful and decorative. Fast growing. Light: bright to moderate shade. Water: 72°–82°F (22°–28°C); pH 6.0–7.8; 3°–18°dH Propagation: runners. Habitat: North America.

Riccia fluitans
Crystalwort

Fast-growing, floating plant; with good fertilizing grows into dense layer; good for spawning. Needs trimming. Light: bright. Water: 59°–86°F (15°–30°C); pH 6.0–8.0; 5°–15°dH. Propagation: divide. Habitat: worldwide.

Vallisneria spiralis

Its leaves are about 15 inches (40 cm) long. Very decorative. Spreads rapidly into dense clumps. Light: bright. Water: 59°–86°F (15°–30°C); pH 6.5–7.5; 5°–15°dH. Propagation: runners. Habitat: tropics and subtropics.

Rotala macrandra
Broad-leaved Rotala

Red-leaved plant for loose groupings; more intensively red with bright light and iron supplements; good contrast for green plants. Not suitable for tank with snails and strong fish. Light: very bright. Water: 77°–86°F (25°–30°C); pH 6.0–7.5; 2°–12°dH. Propagation: plantlets. Habitat: India.

Vesicularia dubyana
Java Moss

It has very fine stems with tiny pointed leaves. Forms thick mat on tank floor, also grows on rocks and roots. Used for egg laying. Light: bright to shady. Water: 64°–86°F (18°–30°C); pH 5.8–7.5; 2°–15°dH Propagation: produces shoots and can be divided. Habitat: Southeast Asia.

Aquarium Plants

Learn the final adult size of each plant before you buy it. A young plant may look small in your dealer's tank, but after just 1 year the same plant may have grown large enough for its leaves to protrude out of the water in your aquarium. When arranging plants in the aquarium, always remember their final sizes and plant them far enough apart not to crowd each other later on. Place the largest plants near the back of the tank; leave the front empty as a space for the fish to swim around freely, or—at most—plant only very small plants there. But do not be too rigid when you decorate your tank, or the various arrangements may look unnatural. Plants with different shapes and colors provide contrast. There is no restriction on creativity and special talents when it comes to decorating the tank with plants as long as no plant is placed in a completely unsuitable environment. For example, the cushion-forming dwarf Amazon Sword Plant grows in shallow water and needs a lot of light. Therefore, it will grow in a deep tank only when a mercury vapor lamp is used. It withers and dies in a poorly lighted, deep—greater than 20 inches (50 cm)—aquarium, or one with colored water.

When you first set up and decorate an aquarium, you are bound to make mistakes. As times goes on, you will probably rearrange some of your plants; just do not remove and replant them too often. They need weeks and sometimes months to overcome the shock and to start growing again. Some species of *Cryptocoryne* need more than a year to adapt to an aquarium. Be patient and do not give up if you have a new aquarium and one of your plants just will not grow.

Transport and Planting

When you buy your plants, they will probably be wrapped in paper or plastic so that they will not dry out; any dried parts will die later in the aquarium. Once home, place the plants in a bowl and cover them with newspaper, which will soak up water and keep the leaves that stick out of the water wet. If you have to wait until the next day for the planting, cover the bowl with plastic wrap or aluminum foil.

Inspect and clean the plants before you plant them. Carefully remove any snail eggs and any wilted, rotting, or broken parts of the plant. Healthy roots are light in color and quite flexible; dead ones are brown, limp, and dried out. With a sharp knife or a pair of scissors carefully trim healthy roots by about one-third (do not bruise them). This trimming stimulates the growth of new roots, which is extremely important because a plant takes up nutrients only with the tips of its roots.

When you are ready to plant, poke a hole in the bottom material and place the plant in it as deeply as possible. Make sure that the root tips are pointing downward. Fill in the hole, and gently press down on the sand or gravel around the plant. Now pull up the plant carefully until the crown of the root is just barely visible. This prevents the root tips from pointing upward, which would make it difficult for the plant to take hold.

Plants such as *Vallisneria* and *Sagittaria* have roots that grow straight downward, and they need narrow, deep holes. Plants of the genus *Echinodorus* have shallow roots and are planted in oval-shaped hollows where the roots can be carefully

Aquarium Plants

spread out. Plants with creeping roots, such as the genus *Acorus,* should be planted on a slant so that their growth areas are not covered with bottom material. *Cryptocoryne* and *Anubias* plants must also be planted in this way; their sprouting spots should not be covered with sand.

When planting ferns, watch out that their green rhizomes (root tops) remain visible above the surface of the bottom material. You can also tie these ferns to rocks or roots, where they can take root. If you have purchased a dormant *Aponogeton* bulb, carefully check from what side its leaves will sprout. If you plant it upside down, it will not be able to grow roots. The "eye" is easily recognized in a healthy, firm bulb; do not buy any products that are bruised, soft, or starting to rot. Remember not to cover the *Aponogeton* root-ball with gravel. *Crenum* bulbs are easily bruised; wrapping them in filter wadding before planting will keep them from being damaged by small pointed rocks or stones.

Stemmed plants such as *Hygrophila, Cabomba,* and *Limnophila* can be bought at larger aquarium stores. Cut off the ends of any lightly bruised stems, and remove all lower leaves up to about 1½ to 2 inches (about 4 cm). Broken stems will not grow; therefore cut off the stem where it is broken and treat the undamaged top part as a new cutting. Stemmed plants should be arranged in groups, but never planted as a bundle. Separate them and plant each one individually to avoid infecting other stems, in case one stem begins to rot.

Place floating plants at the water surface. If they were injured when you brought them home, and roots are tangled around

How to plant aquarium plants:

Clean roots and trim them by about one-third.

Poke a hole in the bottom material and place the plant as deep in it as possible.

Fill in the hole and lightly press down on the sand or gravel (left). Pull up the plant carefully until the crown of the root is just barely visible (right). The root tips should point straight down.

Aquarium Plants

the leaves or stuck to the top side of the plant, just dunk them in water a few times. They will float to the top right side up and free of tangles.

Needs of Aquarium Plants

Plants have adapted to the natural conditions of their original habitats over millions of years. Fortunately, however, most species are flexible and do well even under the altered conditions of an aquarium. Given adequate light, heat, and nutrients, plants will photosynthesize efficiently and produce the greatest amount of oxygen of which they are capable.

Light
Most aquarium plants live in tropical climates and demand quite a lot of sun or other light. Unfortunately, even today many tanks are poorly lighted even though the mercury vapor lamps and tropical lights now available make it possible to produce blossoms even in the most sunlight-demanding plants, such as water lilies and swamp and floating plants. They can thrive in an aquarium without a cover.

As important for plant survival as light intensity is the duration of light. A tropical aquarium needs 12 to 14 hours of light everyday; less time will cut down on plant growth. Use a timer to regulate the lighting time.

Another important factor for plants is the color of the light entering the aquarium. Chlorophyll in plants is activated most by red and blue light, but those colors rarely predominate in common lighting. Also, red light is easily absorbed by water. On the other hand, blue light and green light are best for penetrating water, but green is least effective in activating plant chlorophyll. It is a good idea to add grow lamps (their light has a pinkish violet cast) which will encourage more effective photosynthesis in plants and thus contribute to healthy growth.

Temperature
Plants in temperate climates (Europe and North America) need temperatures between 57° and 68°F (14° and 20°C). Plants grow slower in winter than in summer, even though an aquarium environment ordinarily is not conducive to the customary natural winter dormancy—unless of course your fish need a cold time interval before they spawn. In their natural habitat, these plants go completely dormant during winter (i.e., their vitality decreases and they lose their leaves) and do not produce new shoots again until spring.

Tropical plants grow best in temperatures between 75° and 81°F (24° and 27°C). With the exception of the genus *Aponogeton* tropical plants have no dormancy period. All types of *Aponogeton* live in the area from Madagascar to India to the Malayan Peninsula. They are used to considerable seasonal fluctuations in temperature and water level. If you plant an *Aponogeton* bulb when it is dormant, it will produce shoots, grow for about 8 months abundantly, may even flower if conditions are right and the water level is low, and then will go dormant. If you leave it in your aquarium, it will begin to sprout again within a few weeks but will soon become exhausted and finally die. You will do better to start out by planting

Aquarium Plants

it in the tank in a shallow clay bowl and then removing it from the tank as soon as it begins to go dormant. Now place it in a cool, darker aquarium—temperature at best about 61°F (16°C)—for about 2 to 4 months. After the dormancy period, the plant will again grow shoots at temperatures of 68°F (20°C). If you are willing to be considerate of the particular needs of *Aponogeton*, you will find that it flowers prolifically and is among the most beautiful of aquarium plants.

Required temperature ranges for specific plants are given in the descriptions on pages 52 to 55.

Carbon Dioxide Fertilizing

Plants need carbon dioxide (CO_2) for photosynthesis in order to produce their own building blocks. Since CO_2 is removed from our tap water, aquarium plants often lack a sufficient supply of this gas. As already explained, the occupants of the

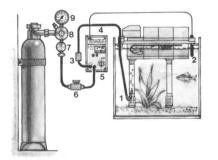

CO_2 fertilizer connected to a filter system. CO_2 leaves the pressurized bottle (the amount released is controlled by an automatic volume control); it moves through the filter unit and into the water. (1 CO_2 connection; 2 pH water; 3 pressure valve; 4 hose; 5 volume control; 6 fine control valve; 7,8,9 pressure reducing units).

aquarium play important roles here: along with oxygen, CO_2 is also dissolved in water, and plants and animals give off CO_2 when they breathe. Plants will benefit from CO_2 in a densely planted aquarium with few fish, where no aeration is necessary. Many tanks, however, are overcrowded with fish, and CO_2 must be removed with strong filtration in order not to endanger the fish. Unfortunately, plants then may suffer, and CO_2 may have to be added as fertilizer, although this is not common.

To provide a balanced supply of carbon dioxide, you may use a CO_2 fertilizer device (a CO_2 diffuser) if you can obtain one. This is a pressurized bottle that continuously gives off CO_2 into the aquarium. The amount of CO_2 released is small and electronically controlled at a constant level. Plants do not take up CO_2 in the dark, but rather release it, so that too much CO_2 fertilizer may endanger fish at night in a heavily populated tank. Therefore, you should add the CO_2 fertilizer device to the same timer that regulates the lighting. The timer will turn off the CO_2 diffuser as soon as the light is turned off.

Since carbon dioxide also enhances root growth, established plants can absorb more nutrients from the bottom sand or gravel, and those newly planted will grow roots much faster. In short, CO_2 fertilizing has substantial advantages. Before purchasing this expensive device, however, you must be certain that you prefer luxurious and abundant plant growth and want to keep only delicate, small fish. If you are not yet sure that you prefer plants to large fish, decorate your aquarium at first with inexpensive, undemanding plants, and concentrate your efforts on learning to keep your fish healthy and happy.

Aquarium Plants

If you finally decide to keep large herbivorous fishes or burrowing cichlids, you will not need a CO_2 diffuser. You should not use CO_2 fertilizer if you keep East African cichlids from lakes Malawi and Tanganyika. A drop in the pH value is unavoidable when CO_2 is added to water, and fishes that have adapted to alkaline water will be harmed. Anyhow, most of these species of fish will eat all the plants in an aquarium.

Fertilizing the Bottom Material

In addition to light and carbon dioxide, aquarium plants need fertilizing salts. The bottom material has to be sufficiently deep and sufficiently light and loose if the fertilizer is to be effective. Bottom soil or gravel should be at least 2 inches (5 cm) deep for a small aquarium and about 3 to 4 inches (8 to 10 cm) for a medium-size or large tank. If you use too much bottom material, even a heating cable or bottom filter will not be able to aerate it well, and it will begin to rot. If, on the other hand, you do not use enough, your plants cannot spread their roots and your swamp plants, especially, will begin to die off.

For your plants to get off to a good start, you should place a long-lasting, time-release fertilizer in the bottom gravel when you first set up your aquarium. Consult your dealer for available products and instructions on how to use them. Long-lasting organic fertilizers are available that contain iron; you mix the fertilizer with a portion of the bottom material and then cover that layer with another layer of washed gravel. Unfortunately, you cannot keep burrowing fishes in an aquarium with an arrangement like this because the water will turn red and cloudy when the fish start to poke around the gravel and dig up the iron-containing fertilizer. There are other granule-type fertilizers that are long-lasting and need not be mixed with the bottom material; they are more suitable for these species of fish. They do not color the water and can be used for all types of fish.

If you use a long-lasting fertilizer in the bottom gravel, you should install a heating pad under the tank or a heating cable in the gravel when you first set up your aquarium. The water needs to flow evenly through the gravel from the bottom upward so that the fertilizer can get to all the plant roots. With any long-lasting, time-release products, you need only use a liquid fertilizer from time to time later on.

If the bottom material has not yet been fertilized, plants can be fertilized with liquid fertilizer or fertilizer tablets carefully pressed into the bottom material near the plants. Swamp plants prefer the tablets; genuine aquatic plants are better off with liquid fertilizer.

For tropical aquarium plants, especially *Cryptocoryne* species, iron is an important nutrient. They normally live in regions where soil is red with iron. If you do not use a long-lasting, time-release fertilizer product, these plants will need a complete fertilizer containing sufficient amounts of iron (consult your local retailer for available products). Using a complete fertilizer for your plants is preferable to using a separate iron product. Theoretically, it is possible to supply iron by putting a metal paper clip in the filter, but often plants suffer gradual injury when an iron fertilizer is used by itself.

The frequency of fertilization and the amount of fertilizer required depend on

Aquarium Plants

the product you buy and vary from one product to another. For this reason it is important to read the directions on the container very carefully.

Fertilize only after you change the water. Fertilizers contain several different fertilizing salts which plants usually use up at different rates. If you keep adding fertilizer without changing the water, the mineral content of the water will gradually be increased. After some time, you will notice that, despite conscientious fertilizing, plant growth leaves much to be desired. Plants do not do well in water that is too high in salts and fertilizer; they will gradually wither and die off.

Care of Aquarium Plants

About once a week remove dead leaves by hand with special tweezers. Using your hands when you work in your aquarium is a much safer and more sensitive method than using any kind of tool. From time to time you should shake off the feathery types of plants if your fish stir up a lot of debris in the tank. The buildup of debris on plant leaves will inhibit photosynthesis. If growth is too rapid, you will need to prune and thin out your plants. If you keep species of *Nymphaea* (water lilies) their blossoms tend to rob other underwater plants of much of their needed light; two to five blossoms are sufficient for a medium-size tank, and all others should be pruned. All floating plants also need to be cleaned occasionally. *Lemna* species (duckweed) grow at such a rapid rate that they will quickly cover everything if you do not watch out. They serve an important function in the water purification system, however, because they absorb oxygen

from the air while at the same time removing nitrogen compounds. Therefore, they do not compete with the fish for oxygen, even in the dark. Plants like *Sagittaria* and *Vallisneria,* which produce vigorous runners, occasionally need to be thinned out by removing an entire plant at one time. If plants such as *Echinodorus* or *Crinum* grow too quickly, carefully pluck or cut off the outer leaves only.

Propagation of Aquarium Plants

Many aquatic plants multiply by means of cuttings, runners, or small plant offshoots. If you want several plants to grow closer together, leave alone the single plantlets that grow next to the mature plant and do not remove the new growth. If you do have to remove a runner, trim it only when it has reached about half the size of the adult plant.

To prevent groupings of plants that multiply by runners from growing too dense, remove some of the weaker young plants. If you do the same with some of the older, unattractive ones, leaving the vigorous younger plants to grow in your tank, you will be proud of your beautiful groupings of *Sagittaria* and *Vallisneria.*

Small new sprouts will form close to the plant above soil level, not from the roots. Several *Echinodorus* species propagate plantlets below the water surface at the whorls of the flowering stems. *Aponogeton undulatus* makes new plants on the flower stem instead of blossoms, and ferns such as *Ceratopteris* and *Microsorium* produce new plants at the edges of their leaves.

Always wait until young plants are strong enough before you take cuttings and plant them. If they have started to grow their

Aquarium Plants

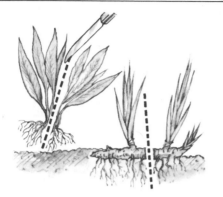

Dividing a grown plant (left) or a root stock (right). A sharp knife is the most suitable tool.

own root system, they will take root faster when they are transplanted. You can also take a runner with young plants growing on it and anchor it in the bottom gravel, either with rocks or plant clamps (check with your pet store for the latter product). Only when young plants have taken root should you separate them from the runner or stem. You can leave the young plants of floating ferns attached to the mature plant; they in turn will form new plants, and soon you will have a dense carpet of floating plants.

You can also increase plants by dividing the root-balls of older, established plants. Divide the rhizomes of ferns and the roots of plants such as *Lagenandra, Echinodorus,* and *Anubias.* Use a sharp knife to cut off a vigorous new shoot, roots and all, with at least five leaves. Now treat the shoot as you would any other young plant. If you have one single, showy plant that has grown too big, cut it in half with a sharp knife, prune its roots, and then replant. A plant that has just had its roots pruned,

however, will be barely able to supply nutrients to its dense crown of leaves. It is possible to cut back the leaves to about one-half or one-third the original size, and that may balance the proportions of leaf-size to root-ball size. Unfortunately, you always take a considerable risk when you divide an older plant: it may either suffer from transplant shock or start to rot along the cut edges. Because of its bulbous rootstock, *Aponogeton* is especially susceptible.

Stemmed plants such as *Ludwigia, Rotala, Cabomba* and *Hygrophila* are easily propagated by cuttings. Use branches of main stems about 6 inches (15 cm) long or the upper parts of stems. Some of these plants tend to be bare at the bottom, even though they grow vigorously toward the water surface or even beyond. Because bare stems look unattractive, you can rejuvenate the entire bunch by lifting it out of the tank, cutting off the tips of a shoot, and replanting it. Or you can have new shoots of stemmed plants grow on the water surface until they have formed their own roots.

Some plants originally lived in swamps or regions that have seasonal fluctuations in the water table. These plants generally flower during the dry season, when they

Catfishes.
Above left: *Pterygoplichthys anisitsi;* above right: Banjo Catfish *(Bunocephalus species);* middle left: Armored Catfish *(Corydoras schwartzi);* middle right: Short-bodied Catfish *(Brochis splendens);* below left: Upside-Down Catfish *(Synodontis nigriventris);* below right: Stripe-tailed Catfish *(Dianema urostriata).*

Aquarium Plants

grow above water. Plants like *Cryptocoryne, Aponogeton, Echinodorus,* and *Crinum* can be propagated in an aquarium by seed. However, growing aquarium plants from seed is usually considered a very special area of expertise for the aquatic horticulturist. If you have an interest in this area, consult literature dealing in detail with the propagation of aquatic plants.

Plant Problems

Plant diseases and deficiencies are rare if plants have good light, necessary nutrients, and clean water. You should, however, check your plants carefully from time to time. Snails and fish may cause minor leaf damage. If you find holes in the leaves or leaf ends chewed off, or if the tips of the leaves of delicately feathered plants are suddenly missing, fish were probably the culprits—provided that your plants are otherwise healthy and growing vigorously.

Other damage to plants or growth problems are generally due to a deficiency of some kind or to overfertilization with specific substances.

• If all or most of your aquarium plants look frail, with yellowish leaves on weak, long stems, they need more light. (Frequently, you will find gravel algae in poorly lighted tanks.) You can encourage vigorous growth in such plants by adding stronger light.

• If plants appear healthy but do not grow, they are probably suffering from carbon dioxide deficiency. Your best bet in this case is to add a CO_2 fertilizer device or to change the water more frequently.

Spiny Eels *(Mastacembelus armatus).*

• If leaves suddenly turn yellow and then look glassy and die off, the plant is suffering from iron deficiency. This can be corrected by fertilizing with iron or, better yet, with a complete fertilizer. (Check for products with your local retailer.)

• Yellow leaves with green veins indicate a deficiency of manganese (not iron). Manganese is a trace element normally present in aquarium water. Manganese deficiency occurs when there is a surplus of iron in the water, or when plants have been fertilized with iron only, not with a complete fertilizer.

• Brown and black discoloration of the leaves usually indicates excessive iron. It is important to remember that iron is a vital nutrient but that it has to be added conservatively to prevent damage to your aquarium plants. Follow package recommendations—do *not* add more than is recommended.

• The plant disease most dreaded in an aquarium is *Cryptocoryne* rot. It manifests itself first by holes in the leaves and around their edges that look as though they had been nibbled by snails or fish. Then, within a few days, an entire plant or *Cryptocoryne* grouping may collapse and rot. Imported plants are especially susceptible; plants propagated locally tend to be less delicate. Some light-green, small-leaved varieties are alleged to be relatively resistant. *Cryptocoryne* rot is caused by an excess of nitrates. Our tap water contains much more nitrates than the tropical waters that are the natural habitat for *Cryptocoryne*. Leftover food particles, decaying pieces of plants, and fish excreta continually add nitrates to the aquarium water. Plants that naturally grow in water high in nitrates can break them down into ammonium,

65

which is a plant nutrient. *Cryptocoryne* and other tropical plants, however, are used to living in water with plenty of ammonium and therefore have not developed the ability to break down nitrates. They take up nitrates just as they do other plant nutrients, but store them with other unusable waste products in their cells. When there is a sudden major change in the aquarium environment, these plants cannot tolerate the shock. (Such a sudden change occurs, for example, when the aquarium hobbyist finally changes the water—a chore long overdue; or, after a long time, adds fertilizer; or replaces an old, worn-out fluorescent tube.) To overcome the shock of the sudden change, the plants reactivate nutrient substances that were stored as reserves and thereby release stored nitrates at the same time. The toxic nitrogen compounds then formed kill the plants.

Plant problems are easily avoided when the aquarium hobbyist
• provides a stable, constant aquarium environment;
• replaces fluorescent tubes regularly to keep the light intensity constant;
• uses a timer to keep the length of daylight constant;
• changes the water regularly to prevent an increase in nitrate concentration;
• follows up each water change with a complete fertilizer, thereby providing plants with all the nutrients they need, but no more.

Algae in an Aquarium

In every aquarium a variety of algae is always present. Like all other plants, algae need light, heat, and nutrients. Generally, they do not compete directly with other aquarium plants as they have different needs with regard to nutrients. In order to thrive, they need considerably more nitrogen than do more complex plants. For this reason they do not do well in a tank with favorable water conditions for fish and for vigorous plant growth. If, however, the water is not changed over a long period of time or the aquarium environment is deteriorating for some other reason, the concentration of nitrogen compounds frequently increases to a level intolerable for more complex plants. The photosynthetic processes slow down, and the plants stop growing. Algae, on the other hand, then multiply rapidly and in very little time will take over the tank. Because of their tremendous growth rate they rob all other plants of light and available nutrients, thereby causing even greater damage and finally killing them.

A new aquarium is most susceptible to this algae damage. Because the filter has not had time to be properly "broken in," the normal breakdown of nitrogen does not yet occur. New plants need time to form roots and grow before they can produce oxygen, take up nitrogen, and thereby help to stabilize the aquarium environment.

Each type of algae is indicative of a specific error in maintaining the water, and therefore algae serve as biological indicators to uncover the causes of problems.
• *Blue-green algae* form a dense blue-green, violet, or brown-black cover on the bottom, rocks, and plants. They particularly favor the bottom, where water does not circulate well. Blue-green algae are also present when the bottom gravel is

Aquarium Plants

overfertilized; other causes are leftover food debris, dead *Tubifex* worms, tap water too high in nitrates, a poorly maintained filter, and oxygen deficiency. You can strip these slimy algae off by hand or siphon them off. Unless you deal first with the cause, however, they will quickly grow back if even a trace of them is left. Leaves attacked by blue-green algae die quickly because of lack of light, and densely covered plants are quite literally suffocated. Unfortunately, fish do not eat them.

• *Red algae* grow in dirty-green threads or beards from plants, wood, and rocks. They are predominantly marine, although there are a few freshwater species. Strong infestation kills the leaves of aquatic plants. Red algae cling firmly to any surface; they are difficult to remove by hand and certainly cannot be siphoned off. They thrive in hard water with a pH over 7 and a high nitrate content. Their presence indicates a lack of carbon dioxide; when this deficiency is corrected, red algae will disappear. Leave them alone, however, and they become just as great a nuisance as blue-green algae.

• *Gravel algae* (diatoms) generally grow in a thin brown layer on decorative objects and plants. Their presence always indicates lack of light, and also inadequate oxygen and excessive nitrogen. If stronger light is supplied, these algae quickly disappear; photosynthesis in plants becomes effective again, and oxygen is produced while nitrogen products are absorbed.

• *Green algae* seldom occur in large quantities in an aquarium. Light-green floating algae of various species, sometimes introduced by adding live food, turn aquarium water into an opaque green brew. Sometimes they appear in newly set up tanks where fish are overfed. These algae will disappear if the light is reduced by a few hours for several days or if the tank gets no light at all. If this is done for a short time only, plants will not be harmed. In a cold-water tank you can add a large number of water fleas (be sure and stop the filter), which will eat the algae. Afterwards, the fattened water fleas are fed to the fish. Unfortunately, this method is not suitable for a tropical aquarium with high temperatures that kill the water fleas and thereby foul the water. In this case a water purifier is the quickest and safest solution; leave it in the tank until all floating algae have disappeared. A number of algae destroyers and water clarifiers available in aquarium stores are effective against green algae.

Other kinds of green algae grow in lush, cotton- or furlike green coats on decorative objects and plants. They indicate water high in nitrates. Remove them by hand or siphon them off as much as possible. Unless you correct the concentration of nitrogen by significantly decreasing it, however, these algae will rapidly grow again.

Green threadlike algae grow only in clean, well-fertilized water where everything is as it should be. Presumably, then, their presence is a good sign. Unfortunately, if allowed to grow vigorously, they form webs around water plants and thus rob them of light as well as nutrients. Delicately feathered and light-hungry plants such as *Cabomba* are quickly killed by green threadlike algae. Remove their long threads by hand, but watch that you do not pull up the plants in the process.

Some species of fish like to eat algae (see page 119). Occasionally, however, the

Aquarium Plants

algae spread so quickly that the fish cannot eat them all or the aquarium hobbyist keep up with them by siphoning. You may then have to use a chemical killer; several effective products are available. Use these products strictly according to instructions, since high concentrations may severely damage or even kill other water plants. Before using the chemical killer, siphon off blue-green algae as much as possible. Once algae have been eliminated, a change of water is recommended.

Important: If all equipment in an aquarium is well maintained, water is changed regularly, and plants are well cared for, algae are not likely to be a problem. When a tank is first set up, you can avoid potential algae infestation by planting a lot of inexpensive but healthy plants. They will grow roots quickly and start photosynthesis. Then algae will not become a problem. After several months you can gradually replace the initial plants with more demanding (and expensive) ones.

Snails in an Aquarium

Every community aquarium has snails that live on small green algae, leftover food, and other debris that fish do not relish. You hardly ever have to buy these scavengers because there are usually some snail eggs on the aquarium plants, or they may get into the tank with live food. Three kinds of snails are well suited for a tropical aquarium:
• Red ramshorn snails *(Planorbis corneus)* are the most popular. Unless there are a great number of them in the aquarium, they are not likely to damage plants. Only plants with delicate and finely feathered

leaves, such as *Rotala indica* or *Cabomba aquatica,* occasionally suffer some damage.
• Malayan snails *(Melanoides tuberculata),* which are live-bearers, usually hide during the day. They burrow in the bottom gravel and surface only at night. They rarely eat plants. Because of their constant

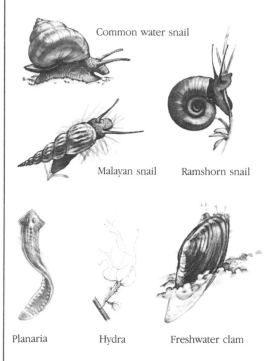

Common water snail

Malayan snail   Ramshorn snail

Planaria   Hydra   Freshwater clam

Invertebrates in the aquarium: Ramshorn snails *(Planorbis corneus)* and Malayan snails *(Melanoides tuberculata)* are for tropical aquariums. The South American mystery snails of the genus *Ampullaris* (common water snails) and freshwater clams are for cold water tanks. Planaria and Hydra (a whitish flat worm) as well as Chlorohydra are sometimes brought into the tank with live foods. They are acceptable in tropical aquariums, but they must be removed from breeding tanks.

Aquarium Plants

digging, debris gets into the bottom gravel, where it fertilizes plants but also contributes to the rotting of the bottom material.

• South American mystery snails of the genus *Ampullaris,* which are distinctive in their beautiful coloring and patterns, grow to almost the size of escargots. They eat fish food and aquatic plants; but, if fed adequately with lettuce, they will rarely harm living plants.

Occasionally mud snails *(Limnaea stagnalis)* are introduced into the aquarium along with live food. This type of snail feeds on plants and may carry diseases. It is difficult to get rid of.

If snails threaten to take over your aquarium, do not immediately purchase a snail pesticide. These chemicals can make sensitive fishes seriously ill. It is far safer to place a lettuce leaf that has been thoroughly scalded and baited with some food pellets in your aquarium overnight. A lot of snails will collect on it and can be removed easily. One lettuce leaf per week or perhaps even per month will probably hold the snail population in check.

On the positive side, snails serve as indicators of poor water conditions before fish show any signs of water deterioration. As long as the snails actively burrow in the bottom, move about the plants, and use their rough tongues to eat trails through the algae coating on the glass, the water is in good condition. If, however, you find the snails lying lethargically on the bottom, with part or all of their bodies withdrawn into their shells, there are toxic substances (by-products of nitrogen breakdown, heavy metals, harmful synthetic materials) in the water. If Malayan snails stop burrowing into the bottom gravel and remaining visible during the day, this is a sign that the bottom material has been depleted. If a great number of snails suddenly die off, it is high time for a thorough chemical analysis of the aquarium water. All snails need calcium to grow their shells and therefore do not do well in soft water.

Types of Food and Feeding

Decades ago an aquarium hobbyist might have gone to a pond or stream once or twice a week, caught some live food such as insect larvae, and fed his or her fish this type of live food exclusively. In this day and age, that is no longer feasible—clean puddles and ponds are hard to come by. Fortunately, commercially available dry food (flakes and tablets) is of such high quality nowadays that most aquarium fishes—the most popular breeder-supplied types—can be fed exceptionally well. Live food is essential only for fishes that feed on it exclusively and for rare imported species that have not adapted to dry food. For fish with such special dietary requirements, specifically bred live food is commercially available. Live food should also be fed to other fish occasionally as a change of pace.

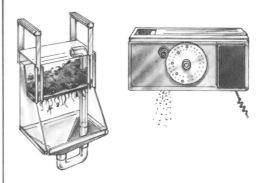

The tubifex storage apparatus at left will keep tubifex worms fresh longer. The automated, timer-controlled device at right can only be used for dried foods.

Food Flakes and Food Pellets

Food flakes and food pellets (dry food) contain not only the necessary nutrients for fish but also sufficient amounts of vitamins, minerals, and roughage (to aid digestion). Because the vitamin content of fish food may decrease in potency when the food is stored over long periods of time, look for the last date of sale, usually found on packages. Vegetable flakes are also available commercially for herbivorous fish.

Food flakes are available in various sizes. Fry and small species of fish require the smallest flakes you can buy. Medium-size flakes can be fed to other fish. Cichlids and other large fish need the larger flakes. Allow food pellets for bottom feeders to float to the bottom. You can leave some food pellets pressed against the glass by applying light finger pressure. Fishes that feed near the center of the tank or close to the water surface will accept these pellets.

Specific foods have been developed for raising young fish—for example, minute bits of powdered food prepared for very small species, or a liquid food substance that resembles the maternal secretions of discus fishes so closely that it can be fed to young discus fish as a supplement. Of course other small fry like it as well. The small fry of large species of fish can be raised on pulverized food flakes of the more expensive kinds, but a more adequate initial food is brine shrimp *(Artemia)* (see page 72).

Live Food

Fish tend to find live food more appealing than dry food because live food moves and wiggles around. Fish have to chase

Types of Food and Feeding

and catch the morsel before eating it. Such food generally stays alive for several hours in an aquarium, and fish see the prey continually appear and disappear. Dry food, on the other hand, sinks to the bottom and there is available for bottom dwellers only.

Since it is easy to introduce disease carriers, especially *Ichthyophthirius* and other parasites, into the aquarium with live food collected in the wild, it is better to obtain live food from water where no fish live. It is safer still to buy live food at a pet shop or perhaps even to raise it yourself (but see page 74).

The most common live foods for fish that you can either buy commercially or catch yourself are as follows:

Red midge larvae (larvae of the midge *Chironomus*) are sometimes available during the winter months. They are quite difficult to catch because they live on the bottom of clear water in the wild. Feed only small portions, even though fish enthusiastically devour them. These larvae immediately sink to the bottom of the aquarium, where they burrow into the ground and are available only to certain kinds of fish, such as loaches and catfish.

Since red midge larvae have tough skins, you should chop them up before feeding them to small fish and fry. They can easily chew their way through the intestine and stomach walls of these fish if they are still alive. Place the chopped-up red midge larvae in a strainer, and rinse well so that their body fluids will not become mixed with the aquarium water.

A small amount of live larvae can be stored in shallow pans in cold water; pour the larvae and water into a strainer and rinse well once more before feeding to your fish. If the weather is hot, the water in the pans must be replaced several times or the larvae will die.

Black gnat larvae are the larvae of various kinds of biting gnats *(Culex)*. You can often catch larvae and pupae during the summer where there is standing water, because they usually stay on the water surface. Black gnat larvae are a favorite morsel for fish that feed at the surface of the water. They are so rich in vitamins and protein that most fish can be stimulated to spawn by feeding with these larvae (pupae are too tough for very small fish). Put just enough larvae in a tank at any one time as can be eaten immediately by its occupants, because black gnat larvae can develop into biting gnats even in an aquarium. Also, remember to cover the aquarium well.

You can sometimes catch enormous numbers of black gnat larvae in flooded meadows, and it pays to freeze what you catch. You can store a small amount of live larvae in cold, shallow water—if possible in containers with large surfaces that provide enough area for all the larvae to stay at the water surface and breathe at the same time. If you place bowls of water outside in the summer, female mosquitoes may lay eggs in them. In a few days you will have larvae. Just be sure to protect bowls or other containers from rain; otherwise, the water will spill over and the precious larvae will be lost.

White midge larvae, which are larvae of the midge *Corethra,* are really transparent rather than white. They normally live only in very clean natural bodies of water and are difficult and quite expensive to buy. Until you are ready to use the mosquitoes for feeding, keep them in cold, shallow

Types of Food and Feeding

water or in a bucket aerated by an airstone. Since they will quickly die in the warm water of a tropical aquarium, you can only use small portions at any one time.

You can also catch *water fleas* during the summer months. These are small crustaceans of the genera *Daphnia, Cyclops, Diaptomus,* and *Bosmina,* which live in many small or large bodies of fairly still, permanent water. These make excellent supplements for dry food, because they keep fish busy, their chitinous shells provide an excellent source of roughage, and their intestinal contents are rich in vitamins and algae. Do not use them as exclusive food, however, for any length of time. Some fish show definite symptoms of deficiency diseases when fed on *Daphnia* exclusively, and other fish prefer to suck out the insides and spit out the hard shells. The bright red *Cyclops* are among the best food on which to raise fry. (But do not feed *Cyclops* to the fry of very small fish species; it is entirely possible for these water fleas to chew their way right through intestine and stomach wall.)

The early stages of small crustaceans are also a good food source for the fry of small fishes. Here, again, is a word of caution: If you offer your fish more than they can eat in a short time, the crustaceans will grow more rapidly than the fish themselves, and some species may, as adults, even attack your fish.

Daphnia are sold live in some pet shops. Like fish, these crustaceans are available in plastic bags with water and a supply of oxygen. If they are not used as food right away, you can store them in a container with well-aerated water for about a day. If you would like to keep them alive longer, or perhaps even cultivate them yourself,

you can place them in about 5 to 10 quarts (liters) of water, aerate the water gently with airstones, and feed them baker's yeast (it is all right if algae grow in this water). Mix the yeast with water, and feed the *Daphnia* a few drops of this solution at a time, just until the water turns cloudy but not until it turns milky. As soon as the *Daphnia* have filtered out the yeast and completely cleared the water, you may begin to feed again. Remember that you will need only small amounts of yeast at a time and that yeast has a tendency to dry out quickly. You can avoid this by cutting a cake of baker's yeast into small pieces and freezing them in several containers. When the *Daphnia* need food, siphon off the contents of one of the containers and let it flow through a strainer. If you want to cultivate another batch, remember to fill the containers with *fresh* water.

Artemia salina (brine shrimp) make an excellent food for growing small fry. Since *artemia* live in salt lakes, they are quite rich in salt. Many pet stores sell live brine shrimp, and the eggs are commercially available in vacuum-packed cans. Take only what you need from the can, and place this portion in a 1 to 2 percent household salt or seawater solution at a temperature of 74° to 80°F (24°C). The eggs will hatch within 24 to 36 hours. Before using them as food, pour them through a strainer. Be sure that you buy only eggs that are guaranteed to hatch (check the package) and that the can is moisture-free. After removing the portion you need, close the can tightly, tape the cover closed, and store the can in a cool, dry place. If you follow this advice, you may find the brine shrimp eggs still viable after 10 years.

Types of Food and Feeding

Do not make brine shrimp the exclusive food for your freshwater fishes, because in time the high salt content will be harmful for them. A one-item diet like this lacks variety and balance, and the fish will soon show signs of deficiency. As growth food

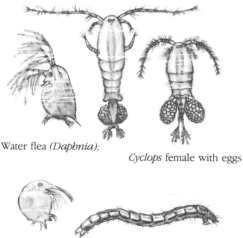

Diaptomus female with eggs

Water flea (Daphnia);

Cyclops female with eggs

Water flea (Bosmina)

Chironomus larva

Corethra larva

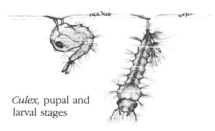

Culex, pupal and larval stages

Live food for aquarium fish. You can catch the kinds shown above yourelf or buy them at the pet store.

for small fry and as a stimulant for adult spawning, however, brine shrimp are unexcelled.

Tubifex, a red, tubelike mud worm, is the most common and cheapest live food available. These worms are also available dried, freeze-dried, and pelletized. They are suitable as a food supplement only, as they neither are very rich in vitamins nor provide sufficient roughage. You can find them in muddy water where fish can no longer live because of the pollution. It follows that there is a considerable danger that this food will introduce diseases into your tank. Before using *Tubifex* worms as live food, place them in a slowly running water for 2 or 3 days until their muddy intestinal contents have been washed away. Once a day carefully lift up the cluster of worms and rinse away the dirt that has collected underneath. *Tubifex* worms die in stagnant water.

Feed these worms in small amounts only; otherwise, they will quickly burrow into the bottom where only catfishes and other bottom feeders can catch them. The quality of the water in the aquarium will deteriorate considerably if you drop a large number of *Tubifex* into it. It is best to shake a small ball of worms with water and then distribute the brew over the surface of the water. This is the most effective method to ensure that the fish will eat most of the worms before they can sink to the bottom.

Earthworms are enjoyed as live food by large cichlids and other large carniverous fishes. Their nutritional value is high enough for fish to be fed an exclusive diet of these worms without showing signs of any deficiency. You can buy earthworms wherever fish bait is sold or dig them up

Types of Food and Feeding

in your own backyard. If you have a compost pile, you can cultivate them there. Before using earthworms as live food, keep them in damp, unbleached paper for a day or two until they have excreted all soil from their intestines and shed their outer mucous membranes.

White worms, such as *Enchytraeus albus* and *Enchytraeus buchholtzi,* and the threadlike eel worms *(Anguillula),* can be grown at home if you can get a starter culture. A lot of work is required to cultivate these worms, and it is not always possible to prevent odors due to the quick fermentation of their food. Most fish love white worms and will gobble them up quickly. Do not give the fish this food too often, however, or let them have too much of it; otherwise the fish will soon suffer from constipation and adipose liver because of the high fat content of these worms— too much is particularly harmful to young fish. On the other hand, eelworms make excellent food for raising small fry.

Cockroaches, crickets, the *common housefly,* fruit flies *(Drosophila),* and similar insects of appropriate size must be especially cultivated for fishes such as butterfly fishes, which live on an exclusive diet of live insects.

As a general rule the cultivation of live food is not worth the effort or the expense. You will do better to buy live food at your local pet shop. You really need live food only if you have fish with special dietary requirements or when you want to breed and raise especially delicate fish. If you have an interest in this field, specialized magazines, journals, and books are available, as well as manufacturers' brochures. You can consult any of these sources for more information about raising live food.

If you either would prefer to raise your own live food, or have no other choice, you should have a space exclusively reserved for this job. You will need a faucet and sink to rinse *Tubifex* worms, as well as electrical outlets for a small refrigerator and other appliances. With this arrangement you won't have to infringe on the space of other family members, nor will it be a major catastrophe if a cricket or cockroach escapes from its box.

Freezing Live Food

If you ever catch or buy more live food than can be used immediately, you should freeze the excess portion as soon as possible. (Worms, unfortunately, do not freeze well—they tend to turn mushy when thawed.) Handle live food pretty much the way you would perishable groceries. Use only a freezer that reduces the food temperature rapidly to the freezing point. This will ensure that the food will retain its nutritional value for 1 to 2 years.

Spread the live food in layers about 2 millimeters thick on sheets of plastic or aluminum foil; then cover with another sheet of aluminum foil. Instead, you can fill plastic bags with the live food, tie the bags at the top, and then press the bags on a level surface to 2-millimeter thickness. Yet another method is to freeze small portions of live food in ice-cube trays. Be sure to label all frozen packages well and, if possible, to keep them in a separate compartment in your freezer. This way you can avoid finding your midge larvae added as spice to your salad dressing some day.

Like perishable groceries, live food, once thawed, must not be refrozen or it will spoil. The frozen sheets of food have to be shielded from heat. If you think that you cannot work quickly enough with your bare hands when breaking off small pieces of frozen food for daily feedings, and there is a possibility that the frozen sheet may thaw, you should wear gloves or use potholders to handle the frozen items. Wait for the food cubes to thaw for a few minutes before placing them in your aquarium.

You can sometimes purchase frozen food for your fish—for example, red and black midge larvae, various types of shrimp, and fully grown *Artemia.*

Freeze-dried Live Food

Besides frozen live food, you can also buy freeze-dried live food at your local specialty shop. Freeze-dried live food contains the same nutrients that are present in the live organisms. It is stored more easily than live or frozen food and keeps for years in a cool, dry place. Unfortunately, freeze-dried food takes a long time to soak up water and gradually float to the bottom of the tank; some fish soon lose patience and no longer pay any attention to it. Presoaking the food before adding it to the aquarium is recommended.

Plant Food

Some fishes, such as certain types of characins and algae eaters, live exclusively on plants, and many cichlids need green plants as a supplement to their diet. If your aquarium does not have an adequate supply of algae, you must feed additional greens to these species. All fishes that either are strict vegetarians or like greens

as part of their diet are especially fond of dry vegetable flakes. Lettuce is also often recommended as a food for such fishes. It has been found, however, that fish stopped spawning if they were fed commercially raised lettuce that had been treated with chemicals; they did not resume spawning until several weeks after removal of the lettuce from their diet. Therefore, feed your fish only lettuce that you can be absolutely certain has been raised organically, without any chemicals or additives.

Fish love young spinach leaves, and you can occasionally get them used to certain plants found in the wild, such as dandelion greens or chickweed. Try to collect them in locations far from highways and industrial centers. Before feeding the leaves, soften them by scalding. Any leftovers not eaten within half a day must be removed from the aquarium, or they will begin to rot and spoil the water.

When and How Much to Feed

How often and how much your fish should be fed will depend on the type and number of fish in your aquarium. Carnivores have large stomachs and tend to gulp down several good-sized morsels of food once a day or only about three times a week. After feeding, they gradually digest their food. Herbivores, on the other hand, have small stomachs but very long intestines. They like to munch on food here and there all day long. Omnivorous fishes and bottom feeders spend the day searching and hunting for food. Fish that are active only at night also feed at night.

If you have a community aquarium, feed fish only two or three times a day and

Types of Food and Feeding

only as much as they can eat within 5 minutes. Sprinkle the food on the water surface so it can spread easily; do not place it in a feeding ring, where it will remain in one area only. In that case the strongest fish will get there first, stake out that territory, and eat to their hearts' content until they have adipose livers, while weaker fish are chased from the territory and end up with no food. All the fish get a chance at the food when it is sprinkled over the entire water surface. Every few days siphon off any food leftovers that have collected at the bottom. If the leftover food particles have dropped all over the bottom, they will not do much harm because all debris will be removed throughout the aquarium when the water is changed.

If you have selected the right combination of fishes for your community tank, they will tend to eat according to a kind of division of labor. For example, fish like pencilfishes swim in an upward, slanted position and feed near the water surface; catfishes search for food near the bottom, and Neon Tetras hunt and catch whatever floats around in the tank. Snails will consume whatever is left. Slow eaters like headstanders need more than the recommended 5 minutes to get enough food. For them you can fasten a food pellet on the glass, or drop it into the tank and let it sink to the bottom. It dissolves gradually, and these fishes can eat until they have had enough.

Food flakes tend to swell up in water, often to three or four times their original volume. Some voracious feeders—for example the Sumatra Barb—gulp their food down so quickly that it does not begin to swell up until it reaches the

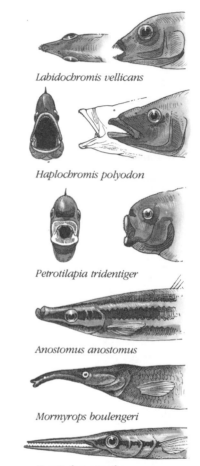

Labidochromis vellicans

Haplochromis polyodon

Petrotilapia tridentiger

Anostomus anostomus

Mormyrops boulengeri

Xenetodon cancila

Mouth shapes tell about the eating habits of fish. *Labidochromis* pick and comb tiny invertebrates from algae. *Haplochromis* hunt fish. *Petrotilapia* scrape algae from stones and rocks. *Anostomus* pick algae from leaves and stones. *Mormyrops* use their trunklike mouths to dig worms and small mollusks and crustaceans out of the mud. *Xenetodon* hunt at the water surface for insects, little frogs and fish.

Types of Food and Feeding

stomach. For this reason it is a good idea to hold onto the food flakes in the water for a few seconds until they have soaked up as much water as possible. Large catfishes are also known to gobble up several food pellets, one right after the other, and you can see them struggle to keep their balance because of their swollen bellies. Trial and error is the best way for you to find out exactly how much food each type of fish can tolerate at one time. With respect to catfishes you can figure on about one-half to one pellet for each 2 inches (5 cm) of fish length.

Better underfeed than overfeed fish! Continually overfed fish get adipose livers and are more susceptible to diseases. Frequently all the fish come rushing to the front glass pane when you approach the tank. If you were to feed them each time this happened, they would soon be overweight. Furthermore, the leftover food would pollute the water because fish are never as hungry as they may appear to you and will never eat all the food you provide. Half-grown and fully grown fish can do without food for a few days. It follows that you can easily leave such fish alone for a weekend. Young fish, however, must be fed daily, sometimes four to six times a day.

You cannot feed your aquarium fish large amounts of food in advance and then not feed them for a long period of time. Food cannot be "stored" in the tank. Unused food spoils, and the water will deteriorate. Live food also dies off within a few hours because of the high temperature in a tropical aquarium.

If you have a powerful filter, shut it off before you begin to feed the fish, but remember to turn it back on when you have finished. Some automatic food dispensers are programmed to take care of this, but they use only dry food. If you feed your fish *Daphnia,* you will have to remember to shut off the filter yourself.

Establishing Fish in the Aquarium and Aquarium Care

What to Watch Out for When Buying Fish

Normally, most species of fish described on pages 114 to 137 of this book are commerically available. Some species, however, have been imported less in recent years and now are available only occasionally or in small numbers. This is due to the Washington Agreement to protect certain endangered species. For example, the Cardinal Tetra (*Cheirodon axelrodi*) is no longer imported all year long.

This catfish digs in the ground and feels for food with his barbels. The tail maneuvers the fish during his ground foraging activities.

A knowledgeable salesperson will be glad to help you with your fish purchases. If you are about to set up your first community aquarium (see page 13), you may want to have a "shopping list" on hand to be sure that you will buy only fish that are truly compatible. Because of the tremendous variety of beautiful fish that is available, it is easy to be tempted into impulse buying, and these spur-of-the-moment purchases usually turn out to be mistakes.

When you select your fish, check the following:
• The fish should not have any small white spots or cotton-like white deposits on the body.
• Their fins must not be fringed
• Their skins should not look dull.
• They should look well fed, but without bloated bellies.
• They should swim actively, but not dart about nervously.
• They should not remain motionless in one corner.

Never buy fish from an aquarium where the water appears yellowish or a fluorescent green or blue. Such discolorations are due to medications and indicate that the fish in the tank are sick.

Transport and Acclimatization

Usually a pet shop will pack the fish you buy in a plastic bag filled with water. There is enough air in the bag for a short trip, but for a longer one (24 hours or more) pure oxygen should be pumped into the bag. Fishes that swim in schools are transported together in a larger bag, but the aggressive cichlids should be packed separately in order to prevent fighting on the way home. Spiny fishes (e.g., catfishes) may puncture plastic bags with their sharp fins, and the water will be lost. It is better to take them home either in mason jars or in small buckets with lids. (Take these with you when you go to buy the fish.) During the cold winter months the plastic bags or other containers should be wrapped in newspaper or, better yet, placed in a Styrofoam box. Transportation is quite a strain on fish, so get your newly purchased pets home as quickly as possible.

Establishing Fish in the Aquarium and Aquarium Care

When you get home with your fish, open the bag and hang it in the aquarium or, better still, in the quarantine tank. You can either use the cover to hold the bag in place or clamp it to the frame with a clothespin so that it will not tip over. Then add aquarium water to the bag gradually, in drops or dribbles, until the water temperatures in the bag and the tank are the same, and your new fish have adjusted to the new conditions. This acclimatization may take no more than 10 minutes for a short trip during the summer months, but an hour or more may be required to equalize the water temperatures in the bag and the tank if you bought the fish during the winter and the water temperature in the bag has dropped significantly.

Your goal must be to avoid any shock due either to temperature change or to chemical changes in the water, when you first establish fish in their new tank. The greater the difference between the water in the bag and the water in your aquarium, the more careful you must be in filling the transport bag with aquarium water—the addition must be done very gradually and cautiously. After you have added approximately the same amount of tank water as was originally in the bag, turn the bag upside down and allow the fish to swim around in their new home. If you do not want the water from the pet store in your tank, you can take the fish out of the bag with a net. Alternatively, you can also place the fish and the water from the bag in a bucket and then add aquarium water as described above. You can place an airstone in the bucket to supply extra oxygen.

If you have bought primarily very territorial fishes, first place the smallest new fish in the tank. After some time, add the next-to-the smallest fish and continue this process, introducing the largest new fish to the aquarium last. In this way unnecessary fights over new territories can be prevented and, more important, small fish have a chance to establish territories or, at the very least, find suitable hiding places. (For the addition of new fish to a group of already established cichlids, see page 133.)

If you have a quarantine tank, place the new fish in it for a few days to see whether there are any signs of disease. Fish that appeared healthy at the dealer's store may be overtaxed by the trip home, and a latent disease may now appear. That is a good reason not to buy new fish before you go on vacation. If you do, the person designated to take care of your fish while you are gone may be suddenly faced with difficult problems.

Care of the Aquarium

Routine Care

Below is a checklist of the duties that you perform regularly in order to create an

The right way to transfer fish to your tank. The plastic bag is opened, hung inside the tank, and slowly filled with water from the tank.

Establishing Fish in the Aquarium and Aquarium Care

aquarium that offers an optimal living environment for its occupants and, at the same time, allows you to enjoy your fish.

Daily Duties

- Feed the fish.
- Check the tank: Is all equipment in working order? Is the temperature correct? Is the water clear and odorless?
- Check the occupants: Are the snails active? Are all the fish present? Do they look healthy? When fed, do all of them eat properly? Are they swimming actively and easily?

Make this quick visual check every morning after the light is turned on and again at noon or at night.

Weekly Duties

- Clean the front panel of the aquarium with a magnetic algae cleaner, a window wiper, or a sponge.
- Check the plants: Are they green and growing well? Are any holes in the leaves caused by snails or by *Cryptocoryne* rot? Are algae beginning to grow in the tank?

Duties Every Other Week

- Check the water for bacteria: Shine a flashlight into the dark aquarium at night. If the water is cloudy because of too many bacteria, the light will look as though it is passing through dusty air.
- Check for the formation of floating algae: If you look into the aquarium from the side, you will quickly recognize even small amounts of these algae before they have reached the pest stage. You can see better this way because you are looking through a deeper layer of water than if you look down from the top.
- Check the chemical condition of the water, particularly the following: pH value (see page 22); nitrite content (see page 23); and hardness (see page 18).

Take immediate action if necessary. Of course, you have to make these checks sooner if anything is obviously wrong in your aquarium at any time.

Monthly Duties

- Siphon off debris.
- Change the water.
- Check filter and clean when necessary.

It is difficult to give a more exact time schedule for these chores. You will need to clean the aquarium more often the more fish you have and the more your fish are fed; this may mean a cleaning job every week or two if you have several large fish. Less frequent cleaning is required—about every 4 to 6 weeks—if you have just a few fish but many plants. If your filter is large in proportion to your tank, you will need to clean it less frequently. Large biological filters can be kept for 6 months to a year.

Disconnect the rod-type heater (pull out the plug) before you begin your cleaning chores. The heater may break if the water level drops while you are siphoning off the debris. A bottom heater may remain plugged in. Turn off any lamps placed on top of the aquarium; if lamps are suspended above the tank, they need not be turned off. Now you can begin cleaning algae and any other deposits off the tank cover. Calcium deposits can be removed with vinegar. Be sure to rinse the cover well before drying it.

Cichlids.
Above left: *Papiliochromis ramirezi;* above right: Flag Cichlid *(Aequidens curviceps);* middle left: Lumphead *(Steatocranus casuarius);* middle right: Pearl Cichlid *(Herichthys cyanoguttatus);* below left: Purple Cichlid *(Pelvicachromis pulcher);* below right: *Lamprologus tetracanthus.*

Establishing Fish in the Aquarium and Aquarium Care

Siphoning off debris: Siphon off debris and water into a bucket with a hose. Place the bucket in front of the tank, put one end of the hose into the tank, and prime the hose briefly at the other end by sucking on it. Before water flows into your mouth, allow the primed hose to drop into the bucket and the water will proceed to drain. Now use the end of the hose that is in the tank like a vacuum cleaner, running it carefully over the bottom of the aquarium and siphoning off the debris, but, if possible, without picking up the gravel. If you have young or very inquisitive fish, you will need to place a net over the end of the hose or you will siphon off the fish as well. That is also the reason for draining the water first into a bucket rather than a sink or the toilet. Just make sure that the bucket does not overflow.

Once the debris has been vacuumed off the bottom, clean the outlets of an outside filter, which take up the water. Often plant particles get caught in them. Finally, you can groom the plants and clean the front glass panel. If blue-green algae have settled in your aquarium, clean all glass panels before draining the water and also carefully remove any algae coating on plants and rocks set into the bottom gravel.

Changing the water: You generally replace about one-third of the water when you siphon off the debris. If, however,

the water has not been changed for some time, replace about two-thirds or three-quarters with fresh water. (You will be able to retain a more stable aquarium environment if small amounts of water—for example, about 5 quarts (liters) for a 55-gallon (22-liter) tank—are exchanged every few days.) Do not exchange a large amount of water every few weeks.

You do not have to heat the water for most fish if it is cold tap water or comes from an ion-exchanger, provided that you allow it to enter very slowly and replace no more than a third of the water. Only discus fishes and similar delicate species do not tolerate a drop in the water temperature very well. In this case it is safer to add water in small amounts at a time. Each time, wait to replace more water until the heater has corrected the water temperature. Of course, it is easier to use tap water of the correct temperature and fill the aquarium with a hose directly from the faucet. Be sure, however, that the water flows slowly and without any pressure; too many air bubbles will agitate the water if the faucet is opened full force. These air bubbles will settle not only on the entire glass surface and on plants but also on your fish. Gas bubbles may form on their skin, their fins, and even in their eyes, causing considerable pain and some killing the fish.

Cleaning the filter: As you have learned, filter bacteria are absolutely necessary to ensure efficient nitrogen breakdown in the tank. Since the number of bacteria is reduced each time the water is changed, it is a good idea not to change the water and the filter material at the same time. Wait about 1 to 2 weeks after changing the water before you clean the filter.

Cichlids.
Above left: Red Top Zebra *Labeotropheus trewavasae;* above right: *Melanochromis johanni;* middle left: *Tropheus duboisi;* middle right: Regan's Julie *(Julidochromis regani);* below left: Orange Chromide *(Etroplus maculatus);* below right: Lyretail Cichlid *(Lamprologus brichardi).*

83

Establishing Fish in the Aquarium and Aquarium Care

To clean your filter, you usually have to take it apart. Because each filter is different, follow exactly the manufacturer's instructions that come with the filter. Discard any filter material like carbon, peat, or very dirty wadding. Materials such as gravel, foam, and small clay tubes may be cleaned and then replaced in the filter. Bear in mind that some of the bacteria must remain on the filter; therefore, clean the filter material with lukewarm, not hot, soapy water (see Filter Maintenance, page 39).

Important Hint: A filter that has not been in operation for several hours, either because of cleaning chores or a defective pump, may be covered with dead bacteria only. In these circumstances toxins develop quickly and may kill all the fish when you turn the filter back on. Be sure, therefore, to clean the filter before turning it on again.

Since major maintenance chores disturb the fish do them only when necessary(i.e., every few weeks). Major cleaning chores should be postponed when your fish are about to spawn.

If it should ever be necessary to clean out your aquarium entirely because the bottom material is rotting (there is a constant slightly bad odor in the water, gas bubbles are rising from the bottom material, samples of the bottom material are black and smell of hydrogen sulfide) and to set it up new, first disconnect all electrical appliances and place the fish in a quarantine tank or in well-aerated buckets. If you use buckets, cover them with towels or the fish will try to escape. Any highly aggressive fishes must be kept separately. Also, place the buckets on Styrofoam pads, instead of a cold floor, to prevent a drop in temperature.

What To Do When Breakdowns Occur

• Some part of the equipment is defective: the filter is not operating, the light is off, the water does not flow, the temperature is too hot or too cold; a motor or a pump is noisier than usual.

Helpful Hint: Turn off the defective equipment, and replace it as soon as possible. A malfunctioning filter or air pump should be replaced the same day.

• The water is cloudy: bacterial flora has multiplied too much because you overfed; the filter is clogged or has stopped.

Helpful Hint: Either replace one-third of the water in the tank or install an ultraviolet lamp that kills bacteria and single-celled organisms. Feed less; clean the filter.

• The water has a foul odor, and foamy bubbles have formed at the water surface or at the filter outlets: nitrogen breakdown is not taking place. You have overfed much too much; fish are dead; the aquarium is new and just set up; a filter has been cleaned too thoroughly and not enough bacteria are present.

Helpful Hint: Immediately change one-third of the water. If necessary, inject the filter with bacteria. If fish have already suffered some damage, transfer them to a clean aquarium.

• Water is clear but gives off a dead-fish odor.

Helpful Hint: Remove the dead fish.

• Snails are motionless and have partially pulled back into their shells; slight poisoning of the water has occurred because of nitrite-or other nitrogen-breakdown by-products, rotting bottom material, heavy metals present in the water, or a toxic substance used to decorate the aquarium.

Helpful Hint: Replace one-third of the

water, and use a preparation to condition the water when refilling the tank. Find and remove the cause of the toxic water.
• Fish are breathing too rapidly, and gasping for air at the water surface: possible causes are nitrite or ammonia poisoning, lack of oxygen, an excess of carbon dioxide, poisoning due to the presence of traces of heavy metal or cleaning solvents, and gill parasites.
Helpful Hint: See Water, page 17; for gill parasites see page 89.
• Fish are darting around the tank nervously: the water is too hot; some type of poisoning has occurred; a rod-type heater is defective and the water is conducting the electric current; one or more pairs of fish are displaying courtship behavior that involves chasing after the other fish.
Helpful Hint: Find the cause and correct it. If courtship is involved, transfer the fish to a breeding tank.
• In an aquarium with aggressive fish, one of these fish is being attacked and bitten.
Helpful Hint: Immediately come to the rescue of the fish.

A mouth fight between two cichlids. Cichlids fight this vehemently quite frequently. Both opponents push and pull with all their might.

The Aquarium During Vacation Time
You should give precise instructions to the person who will take care of your aquarium while you are on vacation. Before you leave, describe in detail how your aquarium should be cared for.

The ideal situation is for your "fishsitter" to join you in taking care of the fish a few days before your departure. In this way he or she not only gets to know the daily chores but also becomes acquainted with the fish and their behavior and learns how many there are altogether and what locations they normally prefer. Tell the caretaker everything that may go wrong and the proper way to deal with breakdowns. Familiarize him with the most important replacement parts, which you will have on hand, and their proper use. Write down everything he needs to know about the daily chores.

Give the caretaker the address and telephone number of your local dealer, whom you have informed of your plans in advance, and also the address and telephone number where you will be staying. You can also leave him this book so that he can look up anything he needs to know.

Another option is a fully automatic operation of your aquarium that will care for your fish for several weeks. This is made possible by a timer, an automatic food dispenser, an automatic heater, and an electronic control center that also measures the necessary water values and corrects anything that is not right. Even then, however, you should have someone check your aquarium at least every 2 days. The electricity might fail or some equipment break down; or your fish may fight, injure or even devour each other, or get sick and die.

Diseases of Fish

Providing correct aquarium care is the surest way to prevent fish from getting sick. Diseases may be caused by viruses, bacteria, and parasites which, in turn, may be of plant or animal origin. Poor water quality and other stresses such as improper diet and water temperature, increase the susceptibility to disease.

Prevention of Disease

As stated above, most diseases can be prevented by proper maintenance.
• Do not overcrowd the aquarium. Crowding is a major cause of stress and leads to parasitic infestation.
• Quarantine newly acquired fish in a separate container for at least 1 week.
• Include in one aquarium only fishes with the same or very similar environmental requirements. If you choose fishes from drastically differing waters (e.g., fishes from mountain creeks, fishes from dark, brackish waters, and fishes from clear lakes), you are programming diseases right into your aquarium. Although clean water and good care may permit fishes of such varying origins to survive, they are not really happy. In case of a sudden alteration in aquarium conditions—due perhaps to a postponed change of water, a slightly clogged filter, a little too much feed— disease will set in quickly. The weakest fish will succumb first, soon the stronger fish will follow, and within a few days all the fish in the aquarium may die. Small fish are stressed severely when they live with large fish, because they are in constant fear of predation. These small fish succumb first to any stress.
• Provide a high-quality filter of sufficient power and clean it regularly. A recirculating pump is appropriate for an aquarium longer than 30 inches provided that the fish (e.g., labyrinth fishes) do not require very still water.
• Bear in mind that many parasites and other pathogens do not like circulating water conditions.
• Maintain the water quality of the aquarium meticulously.

Major Symptoms of Disease

Rocking of body and fin clamping: Signs of general malaise; onset of internal or parasitic disease; water too cold.
Loss of appetite: Intestinal disease; *Ichthyosporidium;* tuberculosis.
Resting on the bottom: Inflammation of the air bladder; tuberculosis.
Headstanding, erratic swimming: *Ichthyosporidium;* tuberculosis.
Gasping for air: Gill parasites; gill rot; ammonia or nitrite poisoning.
Rubbing against objects: External parasites; acid or alkaline toxicity.
Darting about: Parasites; inflammation; water too acid, too alkaline, or too hot.
Dark discoloration: *Ichthyosporidium.*
Red discoloration: Acidity damage; ascites (water in the abdomen).
General paling: Lack of oxygen; poisoning; tuberculosis; chill.
Weight loss: Tuberculosis; other internal diseases.
Bloating: Ascites; tumors.
Bulging eyes: Ascites; tuberculosis.
Protruding gills: Gill parasites; thyroid tumor; lack of oxygen; poisoning.
Spinal and other deformations: Inherited abnormality; aftereffect of tuberculosis.
Fin degeneration: Tuberculosis; bacterial or fungal fin rot.

Diseases of Fish

Bluish-white dulling of the skin: Parasites (e.g., *Costia, Chilodonella*); alkalinity damage.
Skin ulcers: Ascites; tuberculosis.
White dots on the skin: *Ichthyopthirius; Oodinium.*
Whitish, raspberry-like nodules: Lymphocystis.

Poisoning and Other Environmental Disorders

When all the fish in the aquarium suddenly start darting about rapidly, swimming erratically, or gasping for air, you can be quite sure that you are dealing with some sort of poisoning. You can still save the fish by a quick change into a container with correct water conditions, or by a partial exchange of the water they are in.

You must be familiar with chemicals and other products that may cause problems for your fish.

Acids, alkalis, metals: Gills and skins are severely damaged by excessive acidity or alkalinity. Poisoning by heavy metals can be caused by using galvanized buckets, water from new pipes, or water from recently decalcified water heaters.
Prevention: Add a water conditioner whenever you change water. Avoid using for water any containers that you would not use for food storage. If plumbing is new, allow the pipes to clear before you use the water.

Plastics: Many plastic utensils or decorations release into the water phenols or other chemicals that may be poisonous for the fish. Particularly dangerous are objects made of polypropylene and materials containing plasticizers, which are slowly dissolved in the water. The plastic turns slippery at first, then dry and brittle.
Prevention: Check plastic utensils. If, after several hours in hot water, there is still a plastic odor, do not use them. Use hard polyvinyl chloride objects after washing them in 20 percent acetic acid. Before you dump the acid, add some baking soda to neutralize it; acid corrodes chrome in plumbing.

Nitrites: Nitrite poisoning (see page 23) occurs mainly in newly established aquariums. Either the filter is not adequately functioning, or there are too many fish and too much food, or the water is continuously disturbed by cleaning, planting, and other manipulations. On the other hand, if the water exchange becomes overdue, you may get fish with bulging eyes during the course of a day or two.
Prevention: Avoid the causes.

Poisons in your home environment: Poisoning in the aquarium may be due to many environmental causes: cigarette smoke, sprays of all sorts, volatile cleaning agents, and insecticides. Even the pyrethrum-derived insecticides that are usually safe for other animals are poisonous for fish.
Prevention: Cover the aquarium while any of the agents mentioned above is in use. If you want to clean the outside of the aquarium, make sure that nothing spills inside, and remove any residue by wiping all surfaces with clean water.

Spoiled food: No matter how much you paid for the fish food, when it is spoiled it must be thrown out. This goes for live and frozen food. Dry food must be stored away from moisture; otherwise, it will turn moldy. Molds can cause tumors in fish.

Diseases of Fish

Prevention: If you prefer to buy food in large quantities, keep the stored amount in a tightly sealed container. If you use ring feeders, clean them frequently under running tap water, using a brush and paying particular attention to the upper rim, to avoid food rot.

Deficiency Diseases

Causes: Vitamin and mineral deficiencies lead to pale or dark discoloration of the skin and also to generalized weakness. Iodine deficiency results in goiters. *Treatment:* If your standard fish food provides a poorly balanced diet, you must add supplements which you can get through your aquarium store.

Bacterial and Viral Diseases

Bacteria and viruses are ubiquitous, but they will cause disease only in fish that are susceptible because of poor general health.

Fish tuberculosis (TB) is the most common of all bacterial fish diseases. This form of tuberculosis is *not* infectious to people. Almost 80 percent of all aquarium fish carry latent TB infections. They are very difficult to recognize because the symptoms differ from fish to fish. Also, parasites take hold of the weakened fish quickly and conceal the underlying cause. Poor filtration combined with overcrowding is a sure path to TB. Typical symptoms are weight loss, bloody ulcers, gill and fin deterioration, and even spinal and jaw deformation. Although TB cannot be cured, many fish recover from the overt symptoms when the general environment is improved and when secondary infections are treated.

Bacterial fin rot and gill rot are caused by dirty water and water that is too cold.

Infectious ascites is caused by bacteria and/or viruses. Afflicted fish may bloat to the extent that their scales stand up and their eyes bulge. This disease is caused most frequently by poor water conditions or spoiled food. Carps and cichlids are particularly susceptible.

Columnaris (cotton mouth disease) is caused by crowded conditions and poor circulation, and is very contagious.

Lymphocystis is a serious viral infection that mainly affects single cells along the fins. The infected cells grow into nodular, raspberry-like tumors. *Trichogaster,* a large fish of the labyrinth family, is very susceptible to this disease.

Treatment: There is no complete cure for most of these viral and bacterial diseases. However, most specialty aquarium stores will provide you with some type of antibiotic water treatment or food supplements that can be quite effective. For bacterial ascites you can use 100 mg tetracycline or Terramycin per quart of water in a separate treatment aquarium. Check the labels of the brand-name medications for the presence of these antibiotics; they are widely available. After 4 hours' maintenance of the fish in this water, add 50 mg of the antibiotic per quart; after another 4 hours, transfer the fish back into a thoroughly cleaned aquarium. Never treat the maintenance aquarium with antibiotics! They will kill the regular filter bacteria and render the filter ineffective.

You can use antibiotics as a food supplement by mixing small amounts with dried food flakes. If your fish are infected with

Diseases of Fish

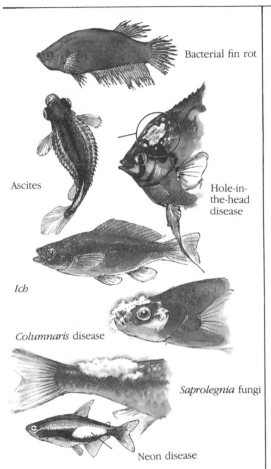

Bacterial fin rot

Ascites

Hole-in-the-head disease

Ich

Columnaris disease

Saprolegnia fungi

Neon disease

Typical symptoms of the most frequent fish diseases: Bacterial fin rot can affect all fishes, but is especially common in Labyrinth fish. Ascites, caused by the bacterium *Pseudomonas,* causes scales to stick out and bulging eyes; it affects mainly catfishes and cichlids. Hole-in-the-head disease, caused by *Ichthyosporidium,* is frequently found in cichlids. White dots are formed by *Ichthyophthirius multifillis,* which is the most common fish disease and affects all fishes. *Columnaris* disease can affect all fishes. *Saprolegnia* is a fungal disease affecting mainly weakened fishes. *Plistophora* causes "Neon Disease" in tetras and other fishes.

lymphocystis and only the edges of the fins are affected, you can try trimming the fins and thereby removing the agent. Only mildly affected fish should be treated; those seriously ill must be destroyed to prevent disaster for all the other fish in the aquarium.

Parasites and Fungal Infections

External parasites are more easily treated than internal parasites and infections because they can be recognized more readily (see drawing, page 89).

Protozoa: These one-celled external parasites are introduced from fish ponds and with fish from other aquariums because of inadequate quarantine procedures. *Ichthyophthirius multifilis,* called "Ich," is the principal offender. Affected fish look as if they are covered with dry Cream of Wheat. There are other parasitic protozoans: *Costia, Chilodonella,* and *Cyclochaeta,* which produce a cloudy skin condition known as the "slimy skin disease"; the head and gill parasite *Trichodina;* the freshwater *Oodinium,* which causes the "velvet disease"; and *Oodinoides vastator,* a long-lived, tough protozoal organism usually imported from Africa.

There are also internal protozoal parasites: they infect other fish after they have been eliminated from the intestines of sick fish into the water, or when a dead fish is cannibalized. "Neon disease," caused by *Plistophora,* affects most frequently the Neon Tetra and other species. The affected fish lose all color and turn white. "Whirling disease" is caused by *Myxosoma;* it causes the same symptoms as "neon disease." A fish with "discus disease" looks as if it has tiny worms on its head.

89

Diseases of Fish

Another internal protozoan, *Hexamita,* affects mainly cichlids. It causes serious disease of the intestine, gall bladder, and liver and is usually fatal, especially under stressful conditions like crowding.

Worms: There are several types of worm parasites. They are also introduced from fish ponds and with live foods. Skin and gill flukes cause breathing distress. Tapeworms and pinworms affect mainly tropical fish. They are recognized only when they protrude from the anal orifice. Another type of worm infestation is the cercaria, an intermediate larval stage; this is rarely a problem because it requires a second host to mature into an adult worm.

Crabs: White crabs in large numbers and sizes can live normally on large indigenous fish. A single, tiny carp-louse, however, is enough to kill a small tropical aquarium fish.

Fungi: Sick and weakened fish are especially susceptible to fungal infestation. *Saprolegnia* and *Achlya* fungi colonize injured skin areas. Fungi accelerate bacterial diseases such as fin rot, tuberculosis, and ascites. When fungal infections occur in fishes already stricken with another disease, death is inevitable.

Treatment: There are many commercially available products that are effective against parasites or protozoans. Most of these are labeled for a specific disease, but they can be effective for others as well. This is true with "Ich" medications, which may be used to treat the "slimy skin disease." "Velvet disease" can be cured with a copper sulfate solution found in most aquarium stores. However, copper sulfate is toxic to plants, so remove the plants from the

aquarium during treatment. In all cases, simply follow the product manufacturer's directions.

Unfortunately, there is no known cure for many internal protozoan infections. If a fish is severely infected, it should be destroyed. Do not flush these fish down the toilet, or put them through the garbage disposal, as you will contaminate the public water system. One internal protozoan, *Hexamita,* can be cured with Flagyl, a prescription drug used on humans. If you can obtain it, you should treat the infected fish every other day with 250 mg per 5 gallons (19 liters) of water; repeat the dose three times.

Flukes can be killed by placing the infected fish in a formalin bath for 30 minutes. This bath is prepared by putting 30 drops of formaldehyde in 1 gallon (4 liters) of water. This dip is also effective against "slimy skin disease." Pinworms and roundworms are killed with piperazine, a puppy and kitten dewormer. Grind up a tablet and place 25 mg of medicine in 10 g of food. For tapeworms, use 50 mg of Yomesan in 10 g of food. These medicines need only be given once.

No known cure exists for most fungal disease. It is best to remove the infected fish immediately. If the fungus has colonized an open wound, swab the area with a 2 percent solution of Mercurochrome or a malachite green solution (1 part in 15,000 parts of water). You can also try some of the "fungus cures" available in aquarium stores.

Killing Fish

It has been mentioned that severely ill fish must sometimes be killed. The quickest, most painless way to do this is by a straight

Diseases of Fish

cut through the neck, severing the head from the body. A sharp knife or pair of scissors is the correct tool, and speed is of the essence. Large specimens should first be stunned by a strong, quick blow on the forehead. It is most important that you learn to act swiftly, since hesitation in your movements will only lead to suffering or painful death. If you do not have the heart or will to kill a sick fish, you should ask a friend who is capable of quick, skillful action, your aquarium dealer, or a veterinarian to do it for you. Flushing a live fish down the toilet is as cruel as drowning cats in a sack. The fact that you will not see the animal die in no way mitigates the cowardice and inhumanity of this method.

The Fish Medicine Cabinet

You cannot protect your fish from all causes of disease. Despite your most careful and thorough procedures, there are potential carriers of germs around your aquarium: flies, splashes of water from other tanks, tools and accessories that are used for several tanks. Fortunately, if you take good care of your fish, they will not be readily susceptible to diseases. Nevertheless, it is advisable to have a basic supply of medication on hand because diseases can occur unexpectedly, sometimes on weekends. If you had to wait 2 days to purchase medication, the disease would be severely aggravated. The following medications are essential: one medicine to treat "Ich" and other protozoal diseases (methylene blue is a good all-purpose choice); one antifungal treatment (any of the proprietary fungicides); and one medicine for diseases specific to your particular fish families (e.g., an agent against *Plistophora* in neon tetras, or against *Hexamita* in cichlids.

In addition, you should keep a disinfectant handy for tanks and for accessories, such as potassium permanganate ($KMnO_4$). You can also prepare a saturated salt solution by adding salt to hot water until the salt no longer dissolves and settles at the bottom of the container.

Important: Most fish medications are colored liquids, or tablets that look like small candies. Keep them out of the reach of children.

Understanding Fish

Evolution of Fish

Fish appear strange to us. Unlike us, they breathe under water. They have an undivided body outline, with no neck, no arms, no legs. Instead of hair, they have scales. There is no external evidence of voice or hearing. However, fish are like us in one very important respect—they too are vertebrate animals. In fact, they are the oldest surviving vertebrates. To the best of our knowledge, fish started their lives in fresh water about 430 million years ago. Later they adapted to ocean waters. Fish fossils have revealed that even the earliest fish forms had the typical vertebrate skeleton: skull, vertebral column, and chest and pelvic bones with jointed ventral and pectoral fins, which correspond to our legs and arms.

Bony fishes (Osteichthyes) have bone skeletons, while Chondrichthyes have cartilaginous skeletons. There is only a single example of cartilaginous fish—the freshwater rays of the genus *Potamotryon* —that is suitable for aquarium life. The largest group of bony fish are the Teleostei, which are of greatest importance to the aquarium hobbyist. This group of bony fish evolved in the oceans around 180 to 130 million years ago. Many varieties adapted to fresh waters. Many new subspecies evolved during the Tertiary ages, about 65 to 50 million years ago. The perches, the labyrinth fishes, and the cichlids all evolved then. From this group many varieties have now been adapted to aquarium life.

The true bony fish constitute the largest group of vertebrates on earth; about 20,000 species are known to exist today. Most of our food fishes, from salmon to herring, belong to this group.

As fish evolved to find their way to the farthest corners of the earth, they had to adapt to many different environmental conditions. Behavioral adaptation is followed, biologically, by physiological and structural adaptations. The fact that fish exist today in the most diverse basic "blueprints" is evidence of their need to develop the body shapes and sensory capabilities required to perpetuate each species in a particular habitat.

Body Shape and Life-Style

The shape of a fish can tell us much about its method of motion and way of life.
• *Streamlined* and *torpedo-shaped fishes* are fast swimmers of high endurance. This group includes many schooling fishes, barbs of the genus *Danio*, and many European river fishes. Laterally compressed fishes are usually quiet and slow, and stay undercover behind plants and stones. Rarely do they swim fast for longer than a moment. Some knifefishes move so carefully that they look as if they were "sneaking" around: they keep their body almost motionless and advance only by the gentle stroke of the hind fin. In this group also are the labyrinth fishes and angelfishes.
• *Round, ball-shaped fishes* (Tetraodontidae) are also slow, and have little endurance. Despite their cumbersome appearance, however, they are highly agile. The body and mouth are specialized for the natural environment and the type of food consumed.
• *Fishes with arched backs, flat bellies, and undershot mouths* are bottom feeders; as the name suggests, they scavenge for food

along and in the bottom material (see drawing, page 76). In this group belong *Corydoras,* the Mormyridae, and the Cobitidae. Some mouths have evolved to veritable snouts to dig in the ground. Bottom dwellers include also fishes that actually dig themselves into the sand. *These fishes are usually flat,* like rays, *or rounded,* like the thorny eels.

Typical surface dweller: *Epiplatys fasciolatus.*

Typical bottom dweller: *Synodontis clarias.*

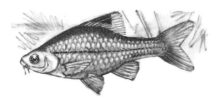

Typical mid-zone dweller: *Puntius dorsimaculatus.*

• *Fishes with flattened backs, and dorsal (back) fins set far toward the tail,* are surface dwellers. Their mouths are set forward and high for the purpose of catching quickly approaching surface feed and insect larvae (see drawing, page 76). In this group are some species of butterfly fish, egg-laying toothed carps, and half-beaks.

• *Fishes of the "normal" fish shapes, with their mouths forming the front tip of the body,* gather their food anywhere in the open water (see drawing, page 76).

Fins

Pectoral and ventral fins are paired and correspond to the legs and arms of land-dwelling animals. Fish also have unpaired dorsal, anal, and tail fins. In addition, some families have adipose (fat) fins, which are located behind the dorsal fins. The fins of bony fishes are supported by bone and cartilaginous raylike structures. The fat fin is not supproted.

The *dorsal fin* may have developed into two, three, or more partitions. In that case the bony, hard sections are in the first section and can often be extended like spines, as in the case of sticklebacks. The dorsal and anal fins are used as stabilizers and rudders for directional control.

The *tail (caudal) fin* is the "engine" that makes all fish move; it has a muscular base for this purpose. A tail fin with sharp cuts or indentations is characteristic of fast, enduring swimmers, whereas slow fishes have fairly straight-edged tail fins. The less defined the tail fin, the rounder or softer in shape, the slower is the fish to which it belongs.

Understanding Fish

The *ventral fins* are used as stabilizers as well as for directional control. They are usually small, and their location varies from fish to fish. Ventral fins may be located anywhere from throat to abdomen to pelvic area, or they may be missing altogether, as on eels. They may even be fused with the anal fin, in which case they are used for forward propulsion.

The *pectoral fins* can be moved forward or backward, or in circular motion. They serve as motor, brake, and stabilizer. Some fishes (e.g., puffers) use their pectoral fins for most of their motion. These fins are not structured with bony rays; rather, they are soft in order to coordinate sensitive directional motions. They are in almost continuous motion, and are characteristi-cally colorless to avoid detection by predators.

Fins have evolved into various specialized structures. For example, ventral fins or anal fin extensions have become a mating organ (the gonopodium) in rays and the Pike Top Minnow. Other specializations are the suction discs of Gobioidei and the "feeler," a sensing and tasting organ evolved from the pelvic fin of gouramis. The anal fin of the live-bearing toothed carps developed into their gonopodium. Some dorsal fins have evolved to contain venomous secretions in individual fin spines, usually in the front sections. Another type of adaptational change is the winglike, spread pectoral fins of some butterfly-fish families and of some mud-skippers.

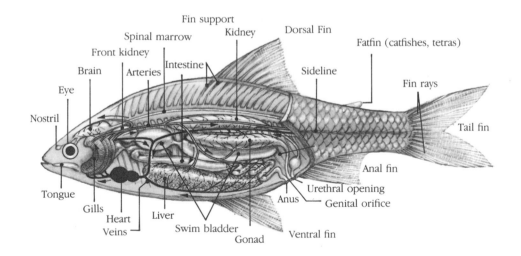

Fish Anatomy. Arrows indicate the direction of circulation. Anatomical knowledge is important for aquarists who intend to learn about the behavior and life patterns of fishes.

Understanding Fish

Skin and Skin Coloration

Like our own skin, the skin of fish has a dermal and an epidermal layer. Unlike ours, however, the top layer of fish skin does not contain horny, sloughing cells; rather it has numerous secretory cells that produce mainly mucus. Some kinds also produce toxins or an "alarm substance" (see page 104). The slippery surface mucus produced by this top cell layer is very important for the quick, smooth motion of the fish. Nerves, blood vessels, scales, and color cells (chromatophores) are located in the dermal layer. The color cells are branched and contain minute color bodies. Many fishes are able to change color with the help of their nervous and hormonal reflex systems.

The coloration of each fish family has evolved so that its protective camouflage colors are those most suitable for the home territory, and its courting colors are the best ones for the native waters and competitors. Thus colors can serve equally for protection and for communication (see page 103). Bottom dwellers are colored to fit their ground environment, but some can also quickly change their colors when they change their habitat. Some angelfishes are striped vertically to fit the roots and stems among which they live. Most fishes have silvery bellies. This serves as protection, since a fish attacking from below will see only a confusingly glistening water surface as it approaches the reflecting silvery belly of the prey. Viewed from the top by a bird, a fish is protected by its dark dorsal surface which is very hard to differentiate from the dark water. On the other hand, *Syndontis nigriventris* swims on its back and therefore has a dark colored belly.

How Fish Breathe

Gills

Most fish breathe through gills. To inhale, the fish opens its mouth, closes its gill covers, and sucks water into the pharynx and gill chambers. When the mouth is closed, the water is pushed out past the gill arches. Here gas exchange takes place with the help of the smallest blood vessels, distributed in the lamellae—the leaflet-like structures that comprise the gills. Oxygen is taken up by these tiny lamellae and distributed to all parts of the body through the blood. At the same time, carbon dioxide (CO_2) is exchanged and removed through the lamellae to the water leaving the gills. Imagine the gill arches and leaves spread out, and you come up with a surface larger than that of the whole fish. The higher the oxygen requirement, that is, the greater the activity of the particular fish, the larger must be the surface area of the gills.

The water temperature also is an important factor in oxygen requirements. Fish, unlike warm-blooded animals, have only one heart chamber, with one prechamber. This means that oxygen-rich and oxygen-poor blood must continuously mix, with the result that fish blood generally is relatively oxygen-poor. In addition, the oxygen requirement increases when the general metabolic rate increases, as occurs when the water temperature rises. Generally, the oxygen content of the water is lower when the water is warmer. Tropical fishes like warm water, unless it becomes warmer than their native temperatures. Then they may experience trouble with breathing. On the other hand, fishes from cool, fast-flowing waters could not survive

Understanding Fish

in warm tropical waters, because their gills would not be able to extract enough oxygen from the warm water. Therefore, as stated previously, it is not feasible to mix fishes of widely different native origins.

Additional Breathing Mechanisms
To enhance their marginal breathing capacity in warm waters, fishes of many kinds have evolved various additional breathing mechanisms to inhale water from above the water surface.
• The simplest adaptation made it possible for the mucosal lining of the mouth to exchange oxygen, as in, for example, the electric eel. For this purpose the mucosal mouth lining has evolved into folds and grooves in order to increase the surface area. In some snakehead fishes and some mud-jumpers, the mouth cavity has developed into a baglike enlargement.
• The intestinal tract can serve as an accessory breathing apparatus. In this case, the terminal intestinal tract is highly vascularized, the oxygen is taken from swallowed water, and the used air is eliminated through the anal opening. The CO_2, however, is eliminated through the gills, as in all other fishes.
• In another adaptation, as in the labyrinth fishes, air is taken into the labyrinth organ, which is a lamellar enlargement of the fourth gill arch. This organ may extend part of the gill cavity into the body cavity under and along the vertebral column. This adaptation can take the shape of paired, baglike structures (in *Heteropneustes*), cauliflower-like appendices (in *Clarias batrachus*), and many other forms.
• The swim bladder also can take on breathing functions, especially in fishes

Labyrinth organ of a labyrinth fish, an example of an additional breathing mechanism.

like carps and salmonids, where it is connected with the intestinal tract. Here, again, the internal surface is enlarged by spongelike folds to accommodate gas exchange. A variation is the evolution of a paired, lunglike air bladder.

The Swim Bladder

The swim bladder of bony fishes lies directly under and along the vertebral column. Filled with CO_2, oxygen, and nitrogen, it serves as a hydrostatic, energy-efficient mechanism to assure suspension in water. The gas mixture adjusts the specific gravity of the fish to compensate for the buoyancy of the water at a given depth. The gas composition changes; therefore, when the fish dives or rises, gases are distributed through the blood and eliminated through the gills and intestinal tract, depending on the specific development of the various fish types.

How Fish Obtain Food

The mouths and teeth of fish vary widely, depending on the food supplies they have adapted to. Similarly, one can tell by the shape and type of mouth and teeth which food was originally natural to each fish.

Understanding Fish

There are very small mouths to eat tiny food like algae and invertebrates. There are also the giant mouths of hunters, some with protrusible jaws, for capturing prey.

The upper and lower jaws of most fish have teeth with single, double, or triple points. The bony pharynx can carry additional sets of teeth. There are also large, inwardly-curved teeth for catching slippery prey such as frogs and fish, and sawed teeth (e.g., the piranha) to tear pieces of meat from prey fish. For plankton and plants, fish need only small teeth; those that eat algae and young growth require scraping teeth. In mollusk eaters the teeth have adapted to be very strong and fused in rows, in order to crack snails and shells. The carps have jaws without teeth but a dentated pharynx.

Lips are also adapted to food intake: some fishes have hardened papillae to scrape up low growth; others (e.g., Loricar-

A specialized form of food procurement. An archer fish *(Toxotes jaculatrix)* shoots water at an insect to dislodge it.

idae, *Hypostomus*) have acquired suction-cup-like lips to adhere to smooth surfaces. The tongue of a fish does not move. Fish do not have salivary glands, which are not needed; land-living vertebrates, on the other hand, require saliva to moisten food before it can be swallowed.

Even the gills are used by some fish to catch plankton by filtering it out of the water. Other adaptations developed for food procurement include extended snouts, large noses like those of stickle-eels, with which they dig and sniff their food, and even mimicry as found in leaffishes (see page 130), and spitting, for example, in archerfishes.

Sensory Organs and Sensory Abilities

Fish sleep with open eyes because they have no eyelids. Fish *eyes* are similar to the eyes of other animals: the lens works like a camera lens, and the iris controls the amount of light by widening the pupil during darkness and contracting it when more light is present. The size of the eyes depends largely on the environment and behavior patterns; fish active during light periods have small eyes. Fish can recognize colors and patterns (see page 103).

Other adaptations to dark and cloudy water conditions are extended barbels, giant eyes, electrical organs, and highly sensitive lateral-line organs (see page 98). There is a Mexican variation of a salmonid *(Astyanax fasciatus mexicanus)* that has no eyes at all, but it has a stronger sensory lateral-line organ and more nerve cells than its sighted counterpart. Those blind cave dwellers also possess a more highly developed olfactory sense.

Understanding Fish

Fish have their *nostrils* situated between the mouth and the eyes on the upper part of the head. There is no connection between nostrils and mouth in bony fishes. Most fish have double nasal orifices: water flows through the front opening, passes by the olfactory mucosal surface, and leaves through the posterior hole. The anterior orifice has a small, sail-like fold of skin that forms a funnel effect. All perches have only a single nasal opening; the movement of the mouth causes the water to enter and be pushed out. The larger the nostrils, the higher is the sensitivity to odors. Little is known about this sensory organ; however, it is certain that the nostrils play an important role in pairing behavior.

Taste buds, if any, are usually situated on the lips, inside the mouth, and on the gill slits. Some fish have tastebuds all over the external body surface. These organs are small groups of sensory cells within the skin.

The *ears* of fish lack an ear drum, as well as external and internal ear canals. This does not mean that fish cannot hear. The inner ear is encapsulated by a bony structure inside the head, where the sensory organ for body balance (see below) is also protected.

The air bladders of some fishes serve as acoustic organs by enhancing sounds. In many of these fish there is a specific opening in the head bone, through which sound waves can travel directly to the inner ear mechanism. Yet another hearing organ is found in fishes such as carps, salmonids, and the American knifefish: the weberian ossicles function by way of three or four small bones that transfer sounds from the bladder into the inner ear. These tiny bones evolved from earlier vertebral structures. It is quite probable that the middle ear of higher vertebrates originated from these tiny bones.

Hearing is usually best in fish that are able to produce sounds. They communicate among their own genus by tones or tone sequences (see page 102).

The balancing organ within the inner ear structure is a cystlike skin formation filled by liquid called endolymph. This organ is composed of three arched, half-moon-shaped ducts that meet in a larger cavity, the otosaccus. The arched ducts contain the sensory cells, which are covered by a gel-like substance. The otolithes, which are tiny calcium-containing deposits, lie on top of minute pillows of sensory hairs. Balancing occurs through the stimulation of the sensory cells, which are excited by the sensory hairs; these, in turn are set in motion by the movement of fluid in the lymph sac each time the fish moves up, down, or sideways. This information system for the brain tells the fish the correct direction of body and movement.

The *lateral-line organ,* found only in fish and in a few primitive amphibians, is a very narrow canal running along the sides, underneath the scales, from tail to head, where it divides into several branches. The lateral-line organ is visible in the form of

Discus and angelfish.
Above left: Blue Discus *(Symphysodon aequifasciata haraldi);* above right: Brown Common Discus *(S. aequifasciata);* below left: Golden Angelfish *(Pterophyllum scalare);* below right: Marbled Angelfish *(P. scalare).*

rows of little holes, which connect the internal gel-like substance with the outside of the scales. The sensory cells inside this canal resemble those of the ear. Single cells of this type are also distributed all over the fish. Waves caused by pressure, like those due to sounds, excite the sensory cells via the gel substance and inform the brain. Therefore the lateral-line organ also serves as a sound and movement detection tele-sensing system: even slight vibrations in the water are registered. For this reason aquarium fish are disturbed and unhappy when people tap the tank walls with their fingers. The single sensory cells on body, lips, mouth, and gill slits register even the minutest impulses.

Sensory organs that sense electricity are also unique to fish; human beings lack them, as they lack the lateral-line organ. Receptors of electricity are specialized sensory organs that can register any electrical impulse in the water. They lie within the skin and are lined with sensory cells. In most fish they are located on the head within a sensory groove. Electric receptors are found in all cartilaginous fishes, and in all fishes that produce electric currents themselves (e.g., the Mormyridae, *Malapterurus electricus, Electrophorus electricus,*

and the American Gymnotoidei). Some fish families have three or more variants of electroreceptors all over the body surface, projecting varying strengths and frequencies of electricity. Such fish perceive, therefore, subtle differences in conductivity.

The electrical organs evolved from muscle tissues as electricity became a necessary adjunct in the refinement of preying, defense, navigation, and family communication. This evolution has proved especially useful in muddy or dark waters.

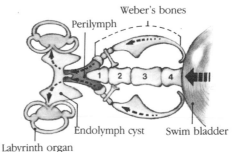

The "Weber Apparatus."
The "Weber's bones" connect the swim bladder with the inner ear and transmit sound. 1–4: Vertebrae from which the Weber's bones evolved.

There are high- and low-voltage fishes. Whereas an electric eel may emit more than 500 volts, a low-voltage fish emits continuous low-grade impulses that create an electric field around the fish. Since any object creates a disturbance of this electric field, the fish "knows," without seeing, that something is near. Electric fishes keep their bodies straight while swimming because their own body movement would otherwise disturb the symmetry of their electric field.

Cyprinids: Barbs.
Above left: Green Barb or Half-striped Barb *(Puntius semifasciolatus);* above right: *Leucaspius delineatus;* middle left: Cherry Barb *(P. titteya);* middle right: Tinfoil Barb *(P. schwanefeldi);* below left: Long-fin Barb *(P. arulius),* below right: *P. eugrammus.*

Understanding Fish

How Fish Communicate

Many ways of communication, as varied as the physical adaptions described above, have evolved among families of fish. Fish send and receive signals utilizing all of their senses: they change color or color patterns, utter sounds, produce electrical impulses, perform ritualized movements, and release chemical signals that can be tasted or smelled. Fish of the same genus, as well as others, understand such "language" and react correspondingly. The aquarium hobbyist can learn enough about these signs for a basic understanding of the subject.

Communication among fish consists mostly of a combination of signals, rather than of only one color or behavioral method. When you begin to understand what the various colors, movements, and other small behavioral changes mean, you will have a better recognition of your fishes' needs. They will, in turn, reward you with good health, magnificent colors, and successful breeding.

Sounds

Little is yet known about fish communication through sound. However, studies with underwater microphones have proved that fish are decidedly not silent—indeed, they are quite "talkative."

Many cichlids and catfishes emit during mating, spawning, or fighting sounds that we cannot hear through our ears. Small salmonid fishes emit and receive almost continuous high-frequency sounds, which may serve to keep schools of fish together. Some of the larger species growl, quack, squeak, or click. Others produce sounds with movements of fin spines against the thorns on their chest fins. The Black Knifefish *(Xenomystus nigri)* "barks" by pushing air through its swim bladder into the intestinal tract. Certain fishes in the Amazon River migrate in large schools during the mating season, at which time the males are as noisy as spectators at a motor-car race. During the spawning season, these males develop muscles that enable them to "drum" on the swim

Electric Eel *(Electrophorus electricus)*

Electric Catfish *(Malapterurus electricus)*

Elephant fish *(Mormyridae)*

Giant Elephant fish *(Gymnarchidae)*

Electrical organs (blackened areas in this drawing). Electrical organs are modified muscle tissue or skin tisue that produce electrical current. The more tissue that has been adapted to produce electrical impulses, the stronger the voltage emitted.

bladder. These muscles involute after spawning.

Some male fishes in coral reefs have recently been shown to emit individual territorial "songs." This sign of territorial occupation is similar to territorial bird singing, and it may well be that the sounds of other fishes are also intended as territorial defenses.

Colors and Movements

Colors and motion are used by cichlids as the primary means of communication. These fish live in pairs and need much "dialog" to correlate their behavior for successful rearing of the young. Many cichlids are striped, with the lowest ranking fishes showing the least striping. Instead of stripes, the lowest ranking fish show intense square patterns on the sides of the body. These squares may disappear or turn into dots or spots—for example, when the fish is being chased and needs color protection. The color characteristics of cichlid parents are different for each genus, and they communicate clearly to other fishes that the brood will be defended at all cost. Also, competitors for food will be attacked, no matter what their size. Such territorial coloring is, therefore, customarily respected by other fishes.

Chemical Signals

Chemical signaling for communication is even less understood than communication through sounds. Scent recognition, however, has been identified in *Ichtalorus nebulosus* from the catfish family. When these fish are allowed to fight and then separated, and the losing fish is later sprayed with water from the tank of the winning fish, the loser will turn pale and hide in the tank. The opposite procedure does not elicit a reaction. Another example of chemical signaling is observed in the cichlid male; he starts courting behavior if water is poured into his tank from a tank where females were kept during egg deposition.

Smell and taste probably play major roles in the mating behavior of many fishes. In fish of the genus *Trichogaster* the ventral fins have evolved into sensing and olfactory organs. If a fish loses its ventral fin by aggression, it also loses the sense of communication necessary to pair successfully, and the result will be disorderly and probably unsuccessful spawning.

Another sign of probable taste sensation is the observation that in many species a fish nudges its male or female partner's mouth toward its genital orifice during spawning.

Electrical Signals

Fish with electrical organs can emit and receive electrical impulses as communication. Not all of these fish communicate for social reasons; many are eager to warn potential trespassers not to enter their electrical field. A potential mating partner, however, will receive less powerful shocks than a nonmating conspecific individual.

Why Fish Fight

Some fishes like to live and hide among plants and stones. However, they must also learn aggressive behavior to defend their territories.

Understanding Fish

Cichlids and labyrinth fishes are fierce territorial defenders. An intruder is confronted by the defender presented lengthwise with extended fins and gill and lowered mouth. Trembling and tail beating follow. This sideways stance of threat is usually effective enough to make smaller fishes retreat. Along the territorial borders the attack is similar but frontal. Aggression commonly ceases just at the most threatening point before contact. This is followed by continued border control. Should a cichlid be found to have intruded far into the territory, it will be surrounded by several fish with extended fins and gills; their tail beating will cause waves to contact the intruder's lateral-line organ and communicate that there is still time to retreat. If the intruder persists, a fight will ensue between it and the largest defender. The fish start biting each other's flanks and mouths; they push and tear each other's fins and scales off. Since there is no escape in an aquarium, the weaker fish will be attacked repeatedly and eventually may be killed. If, however, the weaker fish stops fighting and adopts a submissive position, with the head sideways and toward the tank surface and the body hanging downward, the winner will attack less fiercely and finally stop fighting.

Similar behavior occurs during the mating season, but in this case the females are treated with much less aggression. The males try to lead the females to the spawning locations by exaggerated tail movements. Male fishes that have nipplelike structures for the attraction of partners will repeatedly and deliberately extend their anal fins toward the female while swimming ahead of her toward the spawning place.

Why Some Fishes Live in Schools

The small schools of fish in our aquariums are only a pale reflection of the gigantic schools in the open seas. Most fishes that travel in schools are small and weak as individuals. From the distance a school of fish looks as dense as one very large animal and therefore is not as likely to be attacked. If an enemy does attack, he becomes confused since there are so many prey of the same kind that he cannot quickly decide which one to pursue.

How does a school react when a predator attacks, and even devours, one or more of its members? Some fish families possess an "alarm substance," with an odor, which is released from the skin into the water when tissues are injured in an attack. This phenomenon accounts for the fact that, after a successful attack, schools of these fishes flee instantaneously and avoid the location where the attack occurred for several days subsequently. One can demonstrate this in an aquarium by introducing

Frontal threat by a Firemouth male. The spots on the gill covers make the head appear larger than real; and the bright red mouth is kept open to impress.

freshly injured cell parts into the tank: the school of fish will panic. Strangely, not all school-forming fishes possess this "alarm substance." Among the aquarium fishes several of the barbs, tetras, salmonids, and catfishes release this chemical: *Danio aequipinneatus, Brachidanio rerio, Labeo bicolor, Rasbora heteromorpha, Gyrinocheilus aynonieri, Gymnocorymbus ternetzi, Hemigrammus erythrozonus, Hyphessobrycon innesi, H. scrape,* and *Synodontis nigriventris.*

Not every little scratch will trigger this chemical reaction. Even during catching and transfer, however, a little fish that has been injured can become frightened and stay so, since it does not realize that its own body has released the "alarm substance." In such cases you should consider changing the water to relieve the discomfort of the frightened fish.

In dark- or cloudy-waters the lateral-line organs help the fish to maintain the proper distance from their neighbors in the school. In clear, light waters the bright colors of the fish that swim there enable them to recognize each other, thereby ensuring the integrity of a school. Some fishes (e.g., the Neon Tetra) have small amounts of guanine in their color-carrying cells, which causes light to reflect like aluminum foil.

Breeding Fish

Many aquarium hobbyists are not satisfied with a tank full of beautiful fish—they want to breed them. Often the attempt leads to disappointment when spawning does not occur, or when adults eat their young despite efforts to have correct tank and water conditions. The conditions for the maintenance of fish are quite different from those for breeding. To breed successfully, it is necessary to know, for each fish selected for breeding, the physiological and behavioral characteristics of adults and offspring.

Broadsided threat positions are used by the *Betta smaragdina.*

Sexual Organs

The sexual organs (gonads) of most fishes are invisible from the outside because they lie inside the abdominal cavity. An exception is the male of viviparous and cartilaginous species, where external sexual organs have developed through evolutionary changes in fins. Viviparous fish lay eggs within which advanced stages of embryonic development are found, and cartilaginous fish deposit eggs surrounded by shells. Both the seminiferous and the ovarian ducts lead to a genital papilla that serves for fertilization and egg deposition. Some fish (e.g., cichlids) can actually protrude the papilla slightly for the purpose of spawning.

Understanding Fish

Females develop their eggs in pairs of ovaries, where the eggs are stored until they are ready to be deposited. Some fishes (e.g., East African mouthbrooding fishes) have extra-large eggs rich in yolk, and develop only one ovary because of lack of space for two to develop. Viviparous species have brood pockets inside the ovary or oviduct, where the offspring develops.

Males develop their germinal cells (sperm) in elongated testes adjacent to and below the kidney. The sperm accumulate in a duct or bladder until spawning time.

During the course of the year, the gonads change in size. Fishes in waters of moderate climate have very small gonads during fall and winter. As the days get longer toward spring, and as the water temperature rises, the gonads enlarge with increasing egg and sperm production until they reach their full capacity. Tropical fish, however, reproduce all year long because temperatures do not change greatly. As soon as eggs are deposited and fertilized, the gonads resume their growth. In zones where reproduction is tied to rainy and dry seasons, the gonads are reduced in size during the dry months. These types of adaptation prevent waste of energy in periods when less food is available.

Gender Differences

Since the internally located gonads are invisible, with the exceptions already noted, the aquarium hobbyist must learn to recognize external characteristics of shape and color in order to distinguish males and females. The fish themselves do not, however, rely on external markings; they use scents and other stimulants to identify each other's sex. Fish have had to develop biological mechanisms to recognize not only their own specific breed, and members of the other sex, but also the correct time for reproduction of their own species. In most cases secondary sexual characteristics serve to ensure recognition of a suitable partner. Often these characteristics are strikingly obvious, but sometimes they may be almost invisible. The type and the degree of difference are usually dependent on breed-specific reproductive patterns.

Schooling fishes are usually patterned very similarly to each other as they serve to preserve the integrity of their groups and, therefore, need not recognize individual fish for reproduction. In these groups one can differentiate between males and females only with difficulty. Males frequently have slightly longer fins, and females are a little fatter and slightly paler.

Territorially oriented fishes often show striking differences between males and females. Many of these types stay in pairs for varying durations of time and, as partners, defend the brood and the territory. These fishes show more characteristic individual markings than do schooling fishes.

Males that must compete significantly for a female are usually colorful and often have larger fins with extraordinary colors and patterns (e.g., viviparous and egg-laying toothed carps, labyrinth fishes, cichlids). In these cases the colors proclaim: Get out of my way, fellow males. Female wanted! Males of these species need larger body sizes to ensure a partner and territorial defense of the brood. Among these are the cichlids, the labyrinth fishes, and others characterized by their larger males.

Understanding Fish

In breeds that do not engage in strenuous territorial or competitive fighting, the males are usually smaller than the females (e.g., egg-producing carps).

The characteristics of *brood-intensive fish* depend on the pairing pattern and the duration of the partnership after the eggs are fertilized. Angelfishes are examples of long-paired fish; males and females can hardly be told apart. In these and other pair-forming cichlids the sexes can be differentiated only by the shape of the genital papilla, which is slightly more acute in the male fish. Also, the coloring of the male is usually more intense.

When only one parent cares for the offspring, it would appear appropriate for that fish to be protectively colored to fit the environment. Such is the case with small mouthbrooding females and also with male cichlids that guard the nest and match their coloring to the light-colored sandy ground. However, if a male has finished building the nest and continues to protect it under cover, he can retain all his colorful markings if he wants to attract an additional female.

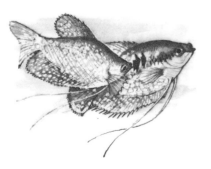

Courting Pearl Gouramis. The partners gently nudge each other's sides with their mouths.

Courting

Courting behavior is a biological mechanism by which mating partners recognize the correct timing for their reproductive activities. During this time, the pair develops behavioral coordination that leads to synchronization of time and place for the deposition of eggs and sperm cells. Since an aquarium is an unnatural environment, it may occur that fishes of different breeds will accept each other as partners. This will lead invariably to short-lived or sterile offspring. In aquariums, killifishes are known to cross freely with related species when conspecific partners are not easily available, because the various female fishes have very similar coloring. This does not occur in open waters because the courting behavior coordinates only species-specific traits. The behavioral patterns of dissimilar species have evolved as different enough, in regard to courting and spawning characteristics, that related species will not cross. In each case the courtship "language" is so well defined that attempts to entice a partner of a different breed will soon be followed by frustration and separation. These mechanisms are essential for the preservation of specific species. If, however, related species are brought together in an aquarium from sources as different as a creek and a lake, the behavioral patterns of these fish may not have developed the barriers of "communication," and crosses of similar fish (e.g., the Platys and the Swordtail) will occur more readily.

Spawning

Fishes that live and spawn in open waters of oceans, lakes, and rivers cannot care for their offspring, many of which are quickly

Understanding Fish

swept away in the plankton. Large numbers of eggs must be produced, since many are also lost to predation. Eggs are usually small, and poor in yolk, since the large number of eggs required for species survival has relatively little space in the female belly cavity. Waters with a wealth of hiding places, such as plants, rocks, wood, or sand, on the other hand, provide fish with secure places for their eggs to be attached, inserted under sand, hidden under leaves, or, as in the case of the bitterling, placed inside clams (see Brood Behavior, page 111). These parent fish have the opportunity to protect their broods, keep the nest clean, and lead the young on outings until they can fend for themselves. Fish in this situation (e.g., mouthbrooders) need fewer eggs to preserve their kind; therefore the eggs can be larger, and richer in yolk. The most efficient brood system is the viviparous type (see page 125).

Most types of fish eggs are fertilized in the water outside of the female body. As soon as a sperm has entered the egg cell, a new fish starts to develop. Some fish eggs hatch after only 1 or 2 days, while others may take months or even years. The cooler the water temperature, the slower is the development. In an aquarium the development of the young can be accelerated by increasing the temperature of the water. This is a risky measure, however, which often leads to quickly hatched, poorly nourished, inadequately colored, and short-finned offspring that are more susceptible to disease than healthier offspring from cooler water. The temperature in a brood tank should never exceed 86°F (30°C) or be kept above the original maintenance temperature for the specific fish.

Development of the Young

Fish and other vertebrates, including human beings, have similar patterns of development. After fertilization, the egg divides first into two, then more and more, daughter cells. The egg of a bony fish divides, not as a whole, but rather only at one pole. The dividing slice at the pole divides into more and then more layered slices, like piled leaves, from which develop the various body parts and organs. Finally, the yolk is enveloped by the germinal layer and thus forms the yolk sac. The first organs to develop are those of the central nervous system, which consists of the brain and spinal cord, followed by the eyes, nostrils, and cystlike hearing organ. Then, appearing to both sides of the vertebral column, are the body musculature, gill slits, heart, and circulatory system. As soon as the head and tail separate from the wall of the egg, they are followed by the mouth and anus. Then the internal organs separate into their final locations. Still later, fins start to bud. Movement begins inside the egg; activity increases, and finally the young leave the egg. The hatching process is made possible chemically through excretion of an enzyme at the top of the embryo's head, which dissolves the membrane of the egg wall. The remaining yolk serves subsequently to nourish the young until they are able to find food in the water.

Planted aquariums.
Examples of suitable plants. Above left: *Hygrophila stricta;* above middle: *Crinum thaianum;* above, foreground: *Saururus cernuus;* below left, background. *Alternantheru reineckii;* below left in front: *Hemianthus micranthemoides;* right front: Cape Fear Spatterdock (*Nuphar* species).

Understanding Fish

In most types of fishes there is a marked difference in the appearance of young and adult. Cichlids, for example, have a larval stage that secretes a sticky substance by which the larvae adhere to the roof of nesting caves or under leaves. When they fall off, the parents pick them up and push them back into place. The secretory glands do not disappear until the young can swim freely and all of the yolk has been consumed. The larval stages of the lungfishes (Polypteridae) develop feathered gills through which breathing is enhanced in warm oxygen-poor water. These larvae look similar to our common tadpoles.

Brood Behavior
You can facilitate successful breeding in the aquarium if you familiarize yourself with the behavioral patterns of fish parents toward their broods and their newly hatched offspring.

Free-spawning Fishes
Among these types of aquarium fishes are the cichlids (Nandidae), some tetras (Tetraodontidae), climbing perches, barbs of the genus *Danio,* and many salmonids. In the natural environment the parents (or a single parent) place the eggs in a protected place—under leaves, on rocks, in the sand, or, as previously mentioned, inside a clam. In an aquarium these fishes

Various fish breeds.
Above left: Longnosed Elephant Fish *Gnathonemus petersi;* above right: *Polypterus ornatipinnis;* middle left: Australian Rainbow fish *(Melanotaenia sexlineatus);* middle right: Stickleback *(Gasterosteus aculeatus);* below left: Archerfish *(Toxotes jaculatrix);* below right: Pumpkinseed *(Lepomis gibbosus).*

strew their eggs throughout the tank and move on without regard for the care of eggs or young. Human intervention is necessary: you must either remove the eggs and transfer them into a brood tank, or separate the parents in a different container.

Fishes That Care for Their Broods
The most interesting brood development is that of many cichlids and labyrinth fishes. The parents of these fish stay in close contact with their young until they are independent. Therefore, these parents and offspring should not be separated unless the parents begin to eat the offspring. One or both parents defend the nest; they use their chest fins to fan oxygenated water over the eggs, and they remove eggs that have been killed by fungal growth or algae. Then they use their mouths to help their young free themselves from the eggs, that is, hatch. Many cichlid parents take the young in their mouths, and then spit them out into little holes that they dug before hatching occurred. The young stick together in the hole because of a sticky secretion which holds them together in clumps. When the young can swim freely, they leave the hole and follow the parents wherever they swim. The parents watch over the swarm of young consistently. They divide the parental duties according to behavior patterns that are different for each kind.

Several types of parenting can be differentiated. These range from totally shared parenting to sole responsibility by one parent.

At one extreme, the male and the female share equally in the care of eggs and young. Both protect, clean, and fan, and

111

Understanding Fish

they stay together as a pair until the young are independent. This type of parenting is found among angelfishes, discus fishes, and colored Indian cichlids.

In another type, the female cares more often, and for longer times, for the young than does the male. Examples are such cichlids as *Cichlasoma nigro fasciatum* and many *Aequidens* species.

Still another type (e.g., *Apistogramma* species and harem cichlids) differentiates parenting roles even further: the male does not stay in contact with the young at all, but is there exclusively to protect the territory.

At the other extreme, parenting is the sole responsibility of either the male or the female. The fish of the opposite sex totally ignores the offspring and their care. Females are the parent among the African mouthbrooders (*Haplocromis, Pseudotropheus, Tropheus,* and many others), while male parenting is prevalent among labyrinth fishes and cichlids. The females of colored cichlids of the genus *Astredinia* sit over their eggs, while other types of offspring attach themselves to folds in the abdominal wall of the mother. The females of other species carry the eggs attached to protrusions at their own hindbody.

Protection of the young is assured by a code of signals that has evolved for communication between parents and young. The offspring are ordered to collect around the parent fish by a sudden characteristic jerking of pelvic, dorsal, and tailfins, by which the fins are first made to stand straight up and then are folded back down. Many cichlids show differently colored abdominal fins during the brooding periods. Mouthbrooders are characterized by dark-colored markings on the head and inside the mouth during parenting: when the parents want the young to return into the mouth, they move their heads toward the bottom, nodding slightly up and down. This is the signal for the young to swim into the mouth cavity.

Getting Fish to Multiply in an Aquarium

Many aquarium owners are disappointed when their long-expected brood finally appears—only to be eaten by the adult fish. This mishap serves no constructive purpose in the artificial conditions of an aquarium; in nature, however, such unplanned egg meals can help to ensure the survival of the consuming fish. When an adult fish finds eggs in free waters, the chances are excellent that they belong to a different genus; consequently, to eat them is not only nutritional but also conducive to the preservation of one's own kind. A competitor is prevented from growing up.

Brood Care. The young discus fishes feed on nutrients secreted from their mother's skin.

Understanding Fish

Blue Acara *(Aequidens pulcher)* in the process of spawning. The female is on the left; the male is on the right.

Females of the viviparous carps are known cannibals. In open waters, however, the newborns can swim away quickly and can hide. If an adult encounters young fish close to her nest, they are, in all likelihood, the offspring of another kind. Also, weak, poorly developed, and sick offspring may stay close to the mother fish, where they are likely to be used as a nutritional protein supplement. This practice leads to a better energy supply for the next brood. There are also behavioral defects, however, that lead to cannibalism. In an aquarium the artificial conditions may sometimes lead to cannibalism among brood-caring fishes, especially if the aquarium is frequently disturbed.

Each genus in itself has good and bad individuals and parents. Nature takes care of serious shortcomings by leading unfit kinds to extinction. In an aquarium, however, for fish that have become commercially successful, brood care is facilitated by human intervention, and less fit individuals can survive. This has happened to angelfishes: their brood-care behavior has become so poor that it is almost impossible to pair them successfully for this role.

Aquarium breeding has led to the sort of domestication of fish that prevents them from being able to survive in open waters; this is true, for example, of many angelfishes, the Guppy, albinos, and radiantly colored fishes. Some of the fancy Swordtails have degenerated to such an extent that they must be fertilized artificially. Nevertheless, they are very beautiful to look at in an aquarium.

Common Species of Fish

Freshwater Rays (Paratrygonidae)

Geographical origin: South America (Brazil, northern Argentina). **Habitat:** Waters over sandy bottoms. **Distinguishing features:** Disc-shaped flattened body; whiplike tail covered with thorny growths that are shed yearly. **Characteristics:** Internal fertilization. The ventral fins of males have evolved into clinging mating organs. Females give birth to live young.

Aquarium care: These fish are not suitable for community aquariums. Very large tanks are most appropriate, since Paratrygonidae reach 15 inches (38 cm) in diameter and 30 inches (76 cm) in length. The floor of the tank must contain at least 4 inches (10 cm) of fine sand, which the fish will dig themselves into during the day. Plants are not recommended since the rays destroy them through their habit of digging in the sand.

Water: Medium hard; slightly acid to neutral. Frequent, efficient filtering and changes of the water are essential. Rays are highly active eaters and are very sensitive to dirty water. **Temperature:** 74° to 78°F (23° to 25°C). **Food:** Preferably live food (earthworms, mussels; insect larvae, fish, fresh or frozen crabs), and commercial food pellets. **Breeding:** To date nothing is known.

Bichirs (Polypteridae)
Photo, page 110

Geographical origin: Tropical Africa. **Habitat:** Muddy waters. **Distinguishing features:** Snakelike, elongated body; the dorsel fin is divided into 5 to 18 tiny finlets. The pectoral fins are modified into armlike structures called lobe fins on which they rest. **Characteristics:** Additional respiratory organs (primitive-type paired lung). These fish must breathe air or they will drown. They are active during dusk and at night and use their acute sense of smell to find food. **Types suitable for an aquarium:** *Calemoichthys calabaricus,* about 35 inches (89 cm) long, and *Polypterus ornatipinnis.*

Aquarium care: These fish are not for community tanks; they need large tanks with much space to swim, soft bottom cover, and dense plant growth. To avoid fighting, plenty of hiding places must be provided.

Water: Medium hard; slightly acid. **Temperature:** 75° to 85°F (24° to 28°C). **Food:** Mainly live food, but they will get used to beef heart and fish meats.

Breeding: The male catches the eggs with his anal fins for fertilization. Do not try to breed these fish unless you are a very experienced aquarium hobbyist.

Freshwater Flying Fish or Butterfly Fish (Pantodontidae)
Photo, page 19

Geographical origin: Western Africa. **Habitat:** Overgrown, slowly moving or still waters. **Distinguishing features:** Surface fish, body shaped like a boat, flat at the top; large upturned mouth and giant pectoral fins; also large tail and anal fins. Pelvic fins are divided into four long, extended rays. **Characteristics:** The butterfly fish (*Pantodon buchholzi*), 6 inches (15 cm), is the only species in this family. Feeds at the surface or hunts for insects "in flight"; the fish jumps out of the water, spreads its large, winglike pectoral fins, and glides over the surface of the water for several yards—in other words, they glide through the air although incapable of genuine flight.

Aquarium care: Butterfly fish are quite aggressive and are best kept in a species aquarium or in a community tank with similar-size bottom feeders. The tank should be spacious, wide, and fairly low, with few plants, although these fish prefer to stay beneath a cover of floating plants.

Water: Soft; slightly acid; needs additional peat or peat filtering. **Temperature:** 77° to 86°F (25° to 30°C). **Food:** Large insects (cockroaches, crickets), mealworms, fish; also frozen live food and large dry food flakes. Feeding them ant pupae stimulates their willingness to spawn. **Breeding:** Before spawning, the male mounts the female's back and rides piggyback fashion for hours at a time, holding onto the female with his pelvic fin rays. When coupling, the fish wrap around each other. The eggs rise to the water surface because of their oil content. Butterfly fish do not take care of their young. The adults spawn for several successive days, and the eggs can be removed from the surface and transferred to a brooding aquarium. Raising the fry is extremely difficult, however, as they accept only the smallest types of live food (aphids, *Drosophila,* etc.). Sometimes they will feed on the young stages of the smallest crustaceans. They need to be continually surrounded by a dense cloud of food because they will eat only whatever floats directly by their mouths.

114

Common Species of Fish

Knifefishes (Notopteridae)

Geographical origin: Western and central Africa; from India to the Malayan Archipelago. **Habitat:** Still, fresh waters. **Distinguishing features:** Body shape resembles that of a knife blade. Small, banner-like dorsal fin (except in the African genus Xenomystus). The caudal fin and anal fin have grown together into one long fin. **Characteristics:** During the day, knifefish will stand motionless (with head pointed downward) in large groups among plants; they feed at night and hunt for small, bottom-dwelling live food such as worms and insect larvae; large types of knifefish prey upon other fish. **Types suitable for an aquarium:** *Xenomystus nigri,* the Black Knifefish, from central Africa, and *Notopterus notoptous,* from Southeast Asia, grow 14 inches (35 cm) long. All other types of knifefish are far too large—24 to 32 inches (60 to 80 cm)—for the average hobbyist's aquarium.

Aquarium care: Knifefish are shy and best kept in a large species aquarium; they will devour small fish if kept in a community tank and usually become quite quarrelsome in a tank that is too small. In spacious aquariums they swim in peaceful, friendly packs. The tank needs dark-colored bottom material and some decorative roots, as well as rocky overhangs; also, dense groups of plants lining the sides of the tank but leaving plenty of space for the fish to swim. Lighting must be dimmed with the help of floating plants.

Water: Soft; slightly acid; peat filtered. **Temperature:** 75° to 82°F (24° to 28°C). **Food:** Primarily live food (worms, insect larvae, fish), also mussel and fish chunks and raw beef heart; sometimes also dry food (the knifefishes have to get used to it). **Breeding:** Knifefish usually spawn along the shorelines on wood and rocks; the male cares for the brood and tends to the fry for several days after hatching. Breeding in the home aquarium is not known.

Elephantfishes (Mormyridae)

Geographical origin: Africa. **Habitat:** Muddy, slow-moving waters. **Distinguishing features:** Most elephantfishes are bottom dwellers. They have a fleshy chin extension in the shape of a finger or an extended, bent, trunk-shaped snout with a tiny mouth. Species with a normal mouth live in open waters. **Characteristics:** Most larger elephantfishes, about 8

to 20 inches (20 to 51 cm), stake out their territories and behave aggressively toward members of their own species, though not toward others. Smaller elephantfishes, about 4 inches (10 cm), usually live in groups. Elephantfish are equipped with weak electric organs in the area of the tail. They have a large brain, and a well-developed cerebellum that controls the coordination of movement. Surprisingly flexible, they are able to swim backward and forward, as well as on their backs or their sides. Elephantfish display a powerful capacity to learn; they are even said to "play" for hours with inanimate objects, such as leaves or empty snail shells.

Aquarium care: Only a highly experienced aquarium hobbyist should keep elephantfish because they require top-quality water and food. They are best kept in a specific aquarium. Although they do not eat other fish and are not bothered by predators because of their electric organ, they are a nuisance for other fish because of their constant electric discharges. For this reason they should be kept either as single fish or with a few fish to each tank. Nocturnal elephantfish need places in which to hide—rocky caves, branched roots, and dense plant growth around the edges and against the backwall. Light must be dimmed with the help of a dense cover of floating plants.

Water: Medium hard; about neutral. Elephantfish can tolerate slightly acid and slightly alkaline water up to 20 dH. On the other hand, they will react adversely to a transfer into water of a different chemical content or into a newly set-up tank. Ideally, they should be kept in a well-established tank (with a stable biological environment), and a water conditioner should be used whenever the water has been changed. **Temperature:** Depending on the geographical origin of the fish, about 68° to 82°F (20° to 28°C). **Food:** Primarily small live food (especially worms), but also food flakes, frozen and freeze-dried food, and occasionally even algae and decayed parts of plants. **Breeding:** To date nothing is known.

Characins and Their Relatives (Characoidei)
Photos, pages 9 and 10 and inside back cover

Geographical origin: About 900 to 1100 species in South and Central America, as well as in Mexico; about 200 species in Africa. **Habitat:** Flowing and still waters; open waters or in dense plant growth.

Common Species of Fish

Distinguishing features: Typical fish shape, scales, and fins, with additional adipose fin behind the dorsal fin. **Gender differences:** Males frequently show somewhat longer, more extended dorsal and anal fins; females acquire a more rounded shape when spawning. **Characteristics:** Almost all characins and their relatives are active during the day and travel in schools. Their bright colors enable fish to identify members of their own species and to keep the schools together. The breeds with luminous markings on their bodies, such as *Cheirodon axelrodi* (the Cardinal Tetra) and *Hemigrammus erythrozonus* (-*gracilis*) (the Glowlight Tetra), live in rivers with clear and black waters. Light-colored and silvery characins swim in bright, clear waters in their natural habitats. The South American white water also contains characins. There is plenty of food there, and larger characins, frequently in huge schools, thrive in this white water. The characins kept in aquariums usually have their origins in rivers with clear and black waters. **Types suitable for an aquarium:** The most commonly kept are the genuine American characins (Characoidea). They have a normal fish shape, more or less flattened sideways, with bright coloring and markings on the sides of their bodies and on their fins; examples are the Cardinal Tetra (*Cheirodon axelrodi*), almost 2 inches (4 cm); the common Neon Tetra (*Paracheirodon innesi*), somewhat less than 2 inches (4 cm); the Black Tetra (*Gymnocorymbus ternetzi*), about 2½ inches (6 cm); the genus *Hyphessobrycon* with the Jewel Tetra (*H. callistus*), almost 2 inches (4 cm) and the Bleeding Heart Tetra (*H. erythrostigma*), almost 2 inches (4 cm); the genus *Hemigrammus,* such as the Rummynose (*H. rhodostromus*), 3 inches (7 cm); also the genus *Moenkhausia;* the Emperor Tetra (*Nematobrycon palmeri*), 3 inches (7 cm), and *Petitella georgiae,* about 3 inches (7 cm).

Various types of the family Serrasalmidae, such as the dangerous piranhas (*Serrasalmus nattereri*), 12 inches (30 cm), and the plant-eating genera, *Mylossoma, Metynnis,* and *Myloplus,* need very large tanks, just to grow to approximately their normal adult size. A brightly lighted aquarium makes them easily frightened and causes them to behave shyly. A hungry piranha will bite members of its own species, and a fish will give off an alarm substance indicating that it is frightened. Therefore a powerful filter and frequent changes of water are essential; otherwise, most fishes will stand motionless in the corners of the tank, continually frightened and very nervous.

Various types of fish from the hatchetfish family (*Gasteropelecidae*) are shy, delicate surface fish and must not be kept in a community tank with more aggressive fish. When they are frightened, they can leap out of the water, and with their large pectoral fins will actually fly through the air as far as several yards.

Various kinds of Lebiasinidae are quite sensitive. The Red-spotted Copeina (*Copeina guttata*), 6 inches (15 cm); the Splash Tetra (*Copella arnoldi*), 3 inches (8 cm); and other *Copella* species are the only characins that care for their spawn (see Breeding, page 117). Among characins and their relatives you can find certain species that have adapted their swimming behaviors to their specific habitats and to the way they take food. For example, the small, shy pencilfish of the genus *Nannostomus* always swim with their heads tilted upward. These are surface fish that feed on mosquito larvae and small insects that have dropped on the water surface. Keep them in a species aquarium only, with high-quality, small live food and dry food flakes, as well as absolutely clear water. Fish of the genus *Thayeria* also swim with their heads tilted upward. Headstanders of the family Anostomidae and the Spotted Headstander (*Chilodus punctatus*), 5 inches (12 cm), on the other hand, stay in the water in a head-down position. In their natural habitat they live among rocks (in rapids), where they pluck off algae and other growth. The Congo Tetra (*Phenacogrammus interruptus*), about 4 inches (10 cm) is the best known African characin.

Aquarium care: Almost all characins and their relatives can be kept in a community aquarium. Exceptions are plant-eating characins and predators such as piranhas and the genera *Exoden, Erythrinus, Acestroamphus,* and *Acestrorynchus,* which are unsuitable for a community tank. Since characins live in schools, you should always buy several fish of each kind, at least 7 to 10, at one time, never just one or two of a species. The smaller characin species will do well even in aquariums no more than 20 inches (50 cm) long. In general, however, characins do not tolerate lack of space and oxygen very well. They thrive and are much happier when you provide them with a longer tank and let them be part of a large school of fish. Also, a larger tank shows these beautiful fish off much better.

Keep in the same community aquarium only species that have nearly the same water and temperature needs. Never mix a lively, vigorous species with smaller, shy, and delicate fishes.

Common Species of Fish

Characins need a large swimming area in the middle of the tank and dense growth along the edges and the backwall, where they can hide when chased. A species needs bottom material of a light color if its natural habitat is bright, light-colored water. On the other hand, fish from clear- and black-water regions require dark-colored bottom material (e.g., gravel or lava rock) and dense plant growth along the edges. Finally, the light must be dimmed by providing floating plants (but no plants in the foreground of the tank).

Water: As low in nitrite and nitrate as possible; soft to medium hard; slightly acid. An efficient filtering system is absolutely essential for all characins: species from clear- and black-water regions need peat filtering. Very delicate and all imported species require a water conditioner when the water is changed. Tap water containing more than 30 mg of nitrate per quart (liter) is not suitable for these fish (remove the nitrate with an ion-exchanger). **Temperature:** Depending on the natural habitat of the fish, 72° to 80°F (22° to 27°C). Characins fall ill quickly when temperatures are too high or when the water has been filtered poorly and is high in nitrates; they quickly become susceptible to "neon disease," caused by *Plistophora*. **Food:** Small-size live food; food flakes. Plant-eating fishes are fed lettuce (if the tank has no plants!), also spinach and dry vegetable flakes. **Breeding:** Most characins do not take care of their spawn. They spawn within their schools or as a couple above dense plant growth or in open waters. For breeding purposes place a pair in a small tank and remove it again after spawning. Characins that do take care of their young are bred in a breeding tank. The eggs are extremely delicate and grow fungi and molds easily; therefore, breeding tanks need to be absolutely clean—preferably disinfected—and must not contain any bottom material or plants.

A very few species of characins, such as *Glandulo candianae,* are characterized by internal fertilization; the males transfer sperm packets to the female, where they are stored in her tubes. The females spawn alone, and eggs are fertilized when deposited. The single sperm deposit can be sufficient for the entire lifespan of the female.

As soon as the characin hatchlings have exhausted their yolk sacs, they must be raised on high-quality powdered food. Unless the water is changed frequently during the growth period, the growth of the young may be stunted.

Carps, Barbs, and Other Cyprinids (Cyprinoidei)
Photos, pages 20 and 100

Geographical Origin: Worldwide, except for South America, Madagascar, and Australia; about 1250 species are in existence. **Habitat:** Still and slow-moving waters; these fish live along banks with dense plant growth, as well as in open waters; only a few species live in cold streams with rapid currents. **Distinguishing features:** Most have one or two pairs of barbels at the corners of the mouth; usually normal fish shape, more or less laterally compressed; normal scales and fins; some types have the typical shape of a bottom dweller. **Gender differences:** Nothing particularly striking; the female is plumper during the spawning period; the male bitterlings (*Rhodeus sericeus amarus*), the Black Ruby Barb (*Puntius nigrofasciatus*), and the Rosy Barb (*P. conchonius*) are generally of more spectacular color during the spawning period than are the females. **Characteristics:** These fishes swim in schools; the slender fish are usually fast swimmers with a lot of stamina; many species are bottom feeders. **Types suitable for an aquarium:** The small species of the original carps (Cyprinidae) are popular, adaptable fish for an aquarium. The Bala Shark (*Balantiocheilos melanopterus*), about 8 inches (20 cm), is a fast, almost perpetual swimmer, suited for a very large, elongated species aquarium (it nibbles at aquatic plants). The small species of the genus *Puntius* (-*Barbus*) are all well suited for a community aquarium, as are Cumming's Barb (*P. cummingi*), about 2 inches (5 cm); the Clown Barb (*P. everetti*), about 5 inches (13 cm); the Black Ruby Barb (*P. nigrofasciatus*), a little over 2½ inches (6 cm); the Checkered Barb (*P. oligolepis*), 2 inches (5 cm); the Half-striped Barb (*P. semifasciolatus*), 2½ inches (6 cm); the yellow variety, known as Schubert's Barb (*P. schuberti*), about 3 inches (8 cm); the Cherry Barb (*P. titteya*), about 2½ inches (6 cm); and the Dotted Barb (*P. tictu*), the variety with more pronounced coloring being known as the Odessa Barb. All of these barbs are peaceful fish that swim in schools and leave their tank mates alone. The Tiger or Sumatra Barb (*Puntius tetrazona*) is not quite as peaceful; it likes to nip off the long fins of angelfishes and labyrinth fishes and even attack the barbels of certain catfishes. These barbs should be kept in a species aquarium. Within their schools ranking orders are established.

Fishes of the genus *Labeo* are suited only for spacious tanks. They resemble loaches in body shape and environmental needs (see page 118). Labeos,

117

Common Species of Fish

especially the Red-tailed Shark (*Labeo bicolor*), 3 inches (8 cm), establish ranking orders. A group of Red-tailed Sharks needs enough hiding places to provide each member with its own refuge. They are not the most peaceful fish when it comes to other species in the tank. Certain barbs, such as the Garrinae varieties, feed on plants and live in fast-moving waters, while the genus *Epalzeorbynchus* is known as an algae cleaner. In order to graze on algae, the lips of these fish are equipped with horny papillae.

The small, elegant rasboras (Rasboridae) are most popular with aquarium hobbyists. They are native primarily to Southeast Asia and the Malay Peninsula. Representatives of the genera *Danio* and *Brachydanio* are small, slim, streamlined fish with longitudinal stripes. They are constantly in motion and excellent at leaping (cover the tank well!) The Zebra Danio (*Brachydanio rerio*), about 2½ inches (6 cm), is one of the most common aquarium fishes. The males of the Giant Danio (*Danio aequipinnatus*) also establish ranking orders in an aquarium. Among the many beautiful fishes of the genus *Rasbora,* the best known is the Harlequin Fish (*Rasbora heteromorpha*), about 2 inches (4.5 cm). Within this genus you will also find some of the smallest aquarium fishes, such as the Pygmy Rasbora (*R. maculata*), 1 inch (2.5 cm), and *R. uruphthalma,* with a spotted tail, about 1 inch (2.5 cm).

Some of the smaller species of North American cyprinids make interesting fish to keep in an unheated aquarium. Several species of dace (*Phoxinus*) and shiners (*Notropis*) may be available in specialty stores or caught in the wild. They are cold-water fish and need clear water high in oxygen. These fish do not burrow, and you can add them to a community aquarium with similar small cold-water fish. Their maximum size is 6 to 7 inches (15 to 18 cm). Consult a guidebook for local species; the Audubon guide has color photographs and useful life-history information.

Aquarium care: Most cyprinids need large tanks with a large swimming area and dense plant growth along the edges. The bottom material should not be too coarse, because almost all species like to burrow (do not use delicate, feathered plants in your tank). Tropical species require dark-colored bottom material. The genus *Rasbora* especially prefers dimmed light, preferably obtained with the help of a loosely floating plant cover. Danios and barbs, however, enjoy some areas of the tank that receive bright light. Do not keep the lively danios and barbs in the same community tank with peaceful, shy fishes. Plant-eating fishes, such as the Tinfoil Barb (*Puntius schwanefeldi*), about 14 inches (34 cm), should not be kept in a community aquarium.

Water: Barbs, algae-eating fish, and danios: soft to medium hard; slightly acid. *Rasbora* species need peat filtering. North American species: medium hard to hard; neutral. Frequent changes of water are required especially for burrowing fishes and voracious feeders, because dirty water makes all cyprinids susceptible to ascites. **Temperature:** Tropical cyprinids: depending on their geographical origin, 72° to 80°F (22° to 27°C). The White Cloud Mountain Minnow (*Tanichthys albonubes*) and the Rosy Barb (*Puntius conchonius*): 64° to 70°F (18° to 21°C). North American cyprinids: 50° to 68°F (10° to 20°C). **Food:** Barbs and certain other cyprinids: small-size live and dry food. Plant eaters: supplemental dry plant flakes, lettuce, and spinach. North American species: live food, some dry food introduced carefully and gradually. **Breeding:** Cyprinids rarely take care of their spawn and young.

Cyprinids spawn on and between plants, to which the sticky eggs adhere. Since most barbs and other cyprinids will eat the eggs, the couple must be immediately separated from their spawn in the breeding tank. Eggs of *Rasbora* species are quite susceptible to fungal infestation; therefore your breeding tank must be exceptionally clean. Depending on the species, the eggs will hatch either within several hours or within several days. After the hatchlings have absorbed the yolk sac, they should be fed high-quality powdered food. When raising small fry, a frequent change of water is necessary to prevent the possibility that the young fish's growth will be stunted.

Loaches (Cobitidae)
Photo, page 20 and back cover

Geographical origin: Europe, North Africa, Asia. The species most frequently seen in aquariums live in Southeast Asia and the Indo-Malayan Archipelago. **Habitat:** Muddy, still waters or clear, fast-moving streams. **Distinguishing features:** Body shape typical of bottom feeders; a characteristically flattened stomach; an overshot mouth; at least three pairs of barbels; a flexible one- or two-pointed spine near each eye that is raised and kept in place while danger threatens. **Characteristics:** Loaches have good

Common Species of Fish

auditory capacity; they may frequently emit croaking sounds that appear important during courtship and when establishing a territory. They have an accessory respiratory organ; if living in oxygen-depleted waters, they will rise to the water surface from time to time and gulp air. Most loaches are nocturnal and hide during the day between rocks, roots, and plants along the banks of rivers. Some loaches form schools when they are still young; young loaches may waste away if kept singly. The adults of some species establish territories and often display aggressive behavior. Virtually nothing is known about the habits of these fishes in their native habitat; therefore, their aggressive behavior, like that of many species of cichlids, may not be the result of lack of space in an aquarium. **Types suitable for an aquarium:** Southeast Asia is the home of the curly-striped, wormlike Kuhli Loach or Leopard Eel (*Acanthophthalmus kuhlii*), which burrows in the bottom during the day. There are several very similar varieties of this species. The most beautiful and colorful loach is the Clown Loach (*Botia macracanthus*), 12 inches (30 cm), from Indonesia. The Dwarf Loach (*Botia sidthimunki*), about 1½ inch (3 cm), is the only species of loach that prefers the middle stratum of the tank. These fish live in schools and are continually on the move.

Aquarium care: Loaches are usually quite shy and need a spacious, peaceful aquarium with plenty of hiding places and not too much light. The bottom material should be soft and of fine consistency since these fish constantly burrow for food with their barbels; coarse bottom gravel must be covered with a thin layer of boiled peat. You can supply hiding places by decorating with wood, coconut shells, rocks, etc. The more nooks and cranies you provide for the fish to hide in, the more relaxed they will be. Finely feathered plants cannot grow in a tank that contains loaches because these fish tend to agitate the water too much, which deposits debris all over the plants. If you keep species that are especially active burrowers, place plants in pots that are buried in the bottom material. If a dense cover of floating plants shades the aquarium, loaches will emerge even during the day. The only loaches suitable for a community aquarium are the Dwarf Loach and a variety of the Kuhli Loaches. All others are too large and too shy.

Water: Soft to medium hard; slightly acid; frequent changes of water, using a water conditioner, are essential. All species are sensitive to nitrates, and dirty water makes loaches susceptible to diseases.

Temperature: Tropical loaches: 73° to 82°F (23° to 28°C); Coolie Loach: 75° to 86°F (24° to 30°C). **Food:** Small-size live food, such as worms and red midge larvae; dry food flakes, or better, pellets. **Breeding:** Breeding loaches in an aquarium is extremely difficult; very little is known about their reproductive behavior in their natural habitats. Presumably, some species move away to special spawning grounds. The Clown Loach spawns at the start of the rainy season in rapidly moving, white water. It is nearly impossible for the aquarium hobbyist to duplicate these environmental conditions.

Algae-Eaters (Gyrilidae)

Geographical origin: Thailand, Borneo. **Habitat:** Mountain streams. **Distinguishing feature:** Wide, overshot mouth with strong lips that enable the algae-eater to anchor on rocks so that it will not be carried along by the rapidly moving streams where it lives. **Gender differences:** During the spawning period, females are larger and plumper than males. Both sexes show an eczematous skin reaction in the snoutlike mouth area.

Aquarium care: The most commonly imported algae-eater is *Gyrinocheilus aymonieri,* 10 inches (25 cm). When young, the algae-eater is a peaceful, vigorous feeder of algae, but the older fish take on territorial behavior and also enjoy feeding on meat. Used to rapidly moving waters, the algae-eater will do well only in an aquarium with strong water circulation and aeration. Provide it with necessary hiding places.

Water: Soft to medium hard; slightly acid. **Temperature:** 72° to 79°F (22° to 26°C); in colder water these fish will stop eating algae. **Food:** Algae, spinach, dry foods from plant and animal sources.

Catfishes (Siluroidei)
Photos, page 63 and back cover

Geographical origin: Worldwide; 2000 species. **Habitat:** Still and moving waters; fish live under rocks, roots, and embankments. Most species in fresh water; a few families (Ariidae, Photosidae) in salt water. **Distinguishing features:** Barbels with sensory cells for taste and touch; usually adipose fins; no scales; naked skin—for example, the bagrid catfishes (Bagridae (-Mystidae)) and the pimelodid or

Common Species of Fish

adipose fin catfishes (Pimelodidae)—or body covered with bony plates—for example, the callichthyd armored catfishes (Callichthyidae) and the suckermouth armored catfishes (Loricariidae). Catfishes that feed by burrowing in the bottom have the common shape of a bottom dweller, with an overshot mouth (Mochokidae; armored catfishes, genus *Corydoras*). Some catfishes hunt fish and other aquatic animals; their shape is long and flexible, and they have wide mouths—for example, bagrid catfishes and labyrinth catfishes (Clariidae). **Characteristics:** Catfishes have a well-developed auditory capacity; many species are known to emit sounds during courtship and when defending their territories. Most catfishes are nocturnal bottom feeders. Because of their nocturnal habits, they have well-developed, strong barbels that enable them to sense and taste food. Catfishes that are active during the day have short barbels. Nocturnal species and species that live in dark or very muddy waters have small eyes. Fish that are active at dusk and live in clear water have normal-size or even enlarged eyes and rely more on vision than other catfishes do. **Types suitable for an aquarium** (in alphabetical order by families):

Bagridae (-Mystidae) (Bagrid or Bumblebee Catfishes): Africa, South and Southeast Asia, and the Indo-Malayan Archipelago. These fish have four pairs of long barbels; the front pair of upper barbels may reach a length more than two-thirds that of the fish itself. Usually only representatives of the genera *Leiocassis* and *Mystus* are kept in a species aquarium. The Barred Siamese Catfish (*Leiocassis siamensis*) normally rests under rocks and plants during the day, generally with its stomach pointed up. It emits not only separate sounds, but also an entire series of sounds. The Indian Catfish (*Mystus vittatus*), 8 inches (21 cm), emits chirping sounds during courtship. Among all bagrid catfishes the females are larger and, during spawning, considerably plumper than the males.

Bunocephalidae: Common in South America. These fish burrow deep into the bottom; only their small, undershot eyes are visible. The most commonly imported fishes are the species of the genus *Bunocephalus*. They are capable of digging up your aquarium plants.

Callichthyidae (Callichthyd and Armored Catfishes): Common in South America. The entire body of these fish is covered with an armor of bony plates. The first ray of the dorsal and pectoral fins is a spine, and the fins are raised and stiffened when danger threatens. With the fins in this position, neither other fishes nor birds can get at the catfish. These fish will burrow for food in groups in sandy banks of rivers or will live in waters overgrown with plant life. If the water is low in oxygen, they use the intestine and hindgut as a supplement-only breathing organ.

Males of the elongated type of callichthyd catfishes, such as *Callichthys callichthys,* 7 inches (18 cm) and of the armored catfishes, such as *Hopiosternum thoracatum,* about 8 inches (20 cm), and members of the genus *Dianema,* build foam and leaf nests underneath the water surface, and they protect their eggs after spawning. Among the Callichthyidae family the armored catfishes (genus *Dianema*) are the most commonly kept catfishes in aquariums. Most fishes of this genus are easy to keep and present few problems for the aquarium hobbyist. Most of these species are nocturnal or active at dusk. Easy to breed are the Peppered Catfish (*Corydoras paleatus*); the Aeneus Catfish (*C. aeneus*), about 3 inches (7.5 cm), and *C. eques.* Unfortunately, these species are not remarkable for their strong coloring. Other species of *Corydoras* are quite colorful, but also much more difficult to breed. There are species with light coloring and black dots and/or markings on their bodies, such as the Saddleback or Black-spotted Catfish (*C. melanistins*), 3 inches (7 cm); the Leopard Catfish (*C. julii*), 2½ inches (6 cm); and *C. schwartzi,* as well as some yellowish and orange-yellowish species with one or several black stripes—for example, the Masked Catfish (*C. metea*); *C. rabouti,* about 2 inches (5.5 cm). The beautiful Reticulated Catfish (*C. reticulatus*), 3 inches (7 cm), is decorated with markings resembling a brown and gold web. Dwarf armored catfishes such as *C. pygmaeus* and *C. hastatus,* about 1½ inches (3.5 cm), swim in schools and are active during the day. They usually originate in open waters.

Among armored catfishes, the female is larger and plumper than the male. During courtship, two or three males pursue one female; one of the males holds onto the barbels of the female with his pectoral fin and then drags her through the aquarium. The female lays one or several eggs into a "cup" formed by the ventral fins, swims through the sperm clouds of the males, and then attaches the eggs to plant leaves that were previously quickly cleaned; or the female may deposit the eggs on the aquarium glass. After spawning, the fish no longer care for the eggs, which can be transferred to brooding tanks, where

Common Species of Fish

they hatch in 5 to 8 days. The young fish are fed extremely small live food and need frequent changes of water.

Clariidae (Labyrinth Catfishes): From Africa to Southeast Asia. The very large "Walking" Catfish (*Clarias batrachus*), 22 inches (55 cm), is an especially voracious predator that hunts fish, frogs, and other small aquatic animals floating along the shoreline. This catfish makes them its prey unless they are larger than one-half its own size. The additional primitive lunglike organs of this species enable it to remain out of the water for some time. This fish will "walk" on land and move on to other areas when the waters it inhabits become dry or are no longer suitable. Only very spacious species aquariums are adequate for this fish, without the company of any smaller catfishes.

Doradidae (Spiny Catfishes): South America. Occasionally, spiny catfishes like to burrow into the bottom sand during the day. Their large heads are very bony, and the gill covers are equipped with spiny protrusions. The lateral lines of the body are armored with bony plates, each plate with a regular or serrated spine, bent backward. The rays of the dorsal and pectoral fins may also be covered with spines and be serrated as well. Some species also carry spiny, bony plates on their backs. When you try to remove one of these fish from the tank, it will raise the spine on its dorsal fin and attempt to squeeze your finger between its pectoral fins and spiny plates. These spines can inflict bloody injuries. Spiny catfishes are nocturnal. They can growl, croak, and quack. If the water is poor in oxygen, they will switch over to their intestinal breathing organs. The spiny catfish that are imported most often are the Talking Catfish (*Acanthodoras spinosissimus*), the Chocolate Spiny Catfish (*Acanthodoras catapractus*), and the Croaking Spiny Catfish (*Amblydoras hancockii*), 6 inches (15 cm). Female Croaking Spiny Catfish have muddy-white stomachs, while the males have brownish white, speckled stomachs.

Ictaluridae (Catfishes): Temperate and subtropical climates of North America. These large catfishes are suitable for a cold-water aquarium. Their wide mouths indicate their ability to prey even on large fish. The Brown Bullhead (*Ictalurus nebulosus*), 18 inches (45 cm), is a handsome species. It is not commonly sold but can sometimes be found. Madtoms (*Noturus*) are smaller and hence more suitable (for cold-water tanks) than are bullheads.

Loricariidae (Sucker-mouth Armored Catfishes): Central and northern regions of South America. The entire body of these fish is armored with bony plates, and the skin is covered with small, toothlike scales. All fins except the caudal fin are reinforced by spines. There are high-backed armored kinds (genera *Hypostomus, Peckoltia*); there are dorsal-ventral flattened kinds (*Loricaria, Ancistrus, Otocinclus*); and there are lance-shaped kinds (*Farowella*). Most species have adapted to life in rapid streams and swift-flowing rivers; others live in large rivers, as far as the river estuaries. The overshot mouth is characterized by powerful "sucker" lips that help the fish to hold onto rocks so that they are not carried along by the strong currents of the waters in which they live. The scraping teeth in the sucker mouth help to shave algae off the rocks. Species of *Ancistrus* (-*Xenocara*) are considered the most effective algae eaters for an aquarium. The gill openings of these armored catfishes are located toward the belly. Once the fish has attached itself firmly with its suction mouth to some object, it will begin breathing through its gills instead of its mouth.

The Bristle-Mouth or Blue-Chin Catfish (*Ancistrus dolichopterus*) is generally kept to remove algae and has occasionally been bred. Sexually mature males develop forked, tentacle-like barbels along the mouth and forehead. Females have either plain barbels or none. They spawn in narrow caves and tight crevices between rocks, and the males take care of the eggs. Males of the armored catfish species *Loricaria* and *Rineloricaria* are remarkable for the barbels around their mouths, as well as the bristle-like skin protrusions on their pectoral fins. Like the *Ancistrus* catfish, they also take care of their spawn. The genus *Otocinclus* is normally found in the central and northern regions of South America. The courtship of the Dwarf Otocinclus (*Otocinclus affinis*), almost 2 inches (4 cm), resembles that of the armored catfishes. The females attach their eggs to glass panes and plants and do not care for their hatchlings. Catfishes of the genera *Hypostomus, Peckoltia*, and *Pterygolichthys* grow too large for the standard-sized aquarium.

Mochokidae (Upside-down Catfishes): Africa. These fish are shaped like large armored catfishes, but the skin is naked and only the head is armored with bony plates. The lower-jaw barbels are feathered. Many of these fishes rest during the day with their heads pointed downward or in an upside-down position among roots and underneath leaves. The Back swimming Upside-down Catfish (*Synodontis*

Common Species of Fish

nigriventris), 6 inches (15 cm), swims and feeds in this inverted position. Like most other types of upside-down catfishes, it lives in groups. These upside-down catfish swim in a normal position during the first few days after hatching and then swim inverted as they mature.

Pangasiidae (Shark-Catfishes): *Pangasius sutchi,* 40 inches (100 cm), is still occasionally imported as an aquarium fish, but these Pangasiidae are by no means suitable for an aquarium. They may grow to more than 3 feet!

Pimelodidae (Pimelodid or Adipose Fin Catfishes): Central and northern regions of South America. These fish are close relatives of the bagrid or bumblebee catfishes (Bagridae) from the Old World. The pimelodids have similar long barbels and a naked skin. Most species live in murky white-water rivers, are nocturnal, and have large eyes. The Polka Dot Catfish (*Pimelodus clarias*), 12 inches (30 cm), is the most commonly imported pimelodid; if water conditions are poor, it can use its auxiliary intestinal breathing organ. It is said that an allergic reaction may result if human skin is punctured by the spine of the pimelodid's dorsal fin, but reports on this effect are contradictory.

Schilbeidae (Glass Catfishes): Africa and India. The African glass catfishes *Eutropiellus debanwie,* 6 inches (15 cm), and *Physailia pellucida,* 4 inches (10 cm), are school fishes that are active during the day. The best place for them is a species aquarium. Their bodies are transparent, but not as transparent as the body of the Indian glass catfish. *Physailia pellucida* is likely to lie on the bottom and "play dead" when disturbed.

Siluridae (True catfishes; Also Known as Glass Catfishes): Throughout Europe and Northern Asia. Among these true catfishes belong the European Catfish, *Silurus glanis,* more than 13 feet (4 meters), and small, very delicate fishes, such as *Krptopterus bicirrhis,* 4 inches (10 cm). The Siluridae are very nearly transparent: the skeleton and the silvery stomach lining that encases the intestines are clearly visible. They are active during the day and swim in small schools that are suspended either in open water or between plants. If you attempt to keep just a single fish, it will waste away. Keep these catfishes in a species aquarium or in a community aquarium with similar small, delicate tankmates.

Aquarium Care: Only armored catfishes (Loricari idae) and the small Upside-down Catfish (Mochokidae) do well in a community aquarium. Catfishes with broad sucker mouths and well-developed barbels are generally successful predators that will easily find and catch their own live food in a community aquarium. Neither a school of fish nor single fishes of many of the other species inhabiting a community tank will be safe from them. Suitable for a species aquarium are the larger species of *Clarias* (Clariidae), the *Leiocassis* species, and *Mystus vittatus* (Bagridae), as well as the pimelodids (Pimelodidae).

All catfishes need hiding places in an aquarium where they can spend the day; even catfishes that are active during the day like to rest under plant leaves from time to time. Depending on the size of your fish, you can build refuges for them with rocks and piles of flagstones (see drawing, page 47), or use tree roots or coconut shells.

Some catfishes prefer to stay among dense plant growth. For burrowing catfishes (e.g., spiny catfishes) and for bottom feeders (e.g., armored catfishes) the bottom sand must be soft; cover coarse gravel with a thin layer of soft bottom material. If you keep larger species of catfishes, forget about delicate or feathery-leafed plants in your aquarium. Only catfishes of the genera *Corydoras* and *Otoclincus* will refrain from agitating the water excessively, so that less debris will float about and settle on the plants.

Water: Soft to slightly acid, except for Ictaluridae, which require medium-hard to hard, neutral water. Species from black- and clear-water regions need peat filtering; all catfishes require a strong filtering system. For most catfishes the water must be very clean. Especially sensitive to nitrates are such catfishes as the Indian and African glass catfishes, the Pimelodidae, the Mochokidae, the Loricariidae, and catfishes of the genus *Dianema*. These fishes (especially imported varieties) need frequent changes of water and water of very high quality. Loricariidae that have adapted to life in very strong currents require strong water circulation, achieved by using a turbo water pump. A strong water current is also recommended for Indian and African glass catfish species. **Temperature:** Depending on the origin of the fish, 72° to 100°F (22° to 38°C). Some species from the southern parts of South America, such as *Corydoras paleatus,* 3 inches (8 cm), as well as species from river estuaries, such as *Loricaria* and *Rimeloricaria* varieties: 72° to 77°F (22° to 24°C). Mochokidae catfishes from central Africa: 79° to 82°F (26° to 28°C). **Food:** Live food (*Tubifex* worms, red midge larvae) and dry food (preferably pellets). Remember to feed nocturnal catfishes in the evening! Large catfishes need big pieces of live food; get them used to chunks of fish and beef heart. Clariidae and mature catfishes of other families will also eat small, live freshwater fish that you can buy either at a pet shop or wherever bait is sold for fishing. **Breeding:** Breeding catfishes is quite difficult; they will rarely spawn in a community tank, and therefore you will need special species tanks. Unlike characins and barbs, these fish cannot be bred at will. However, some factors will increase their willingness to mate and spawn, such as feeding them red midge larvae or raising the water temperature by 2° to 5°F (1° to 3°C). Varieties such as *Hoplosternum thoractum,* 8 inches (20 cm), and *Callichthys callichthys* will spawn when the water temperature is raised, and you can duplicate the rainy season of their natural habitat by replacing about two-thirds of the tank water with water that has had all minerals removed. When you add the soft water, be sure to use a watering can with a type of shower head from which the water falls like a gentle fountain. Do not use either a bucket or a hose.

When the young have hatched and eaten the yolk sac, transfer them to a special tank set up specifically for raising small fry. Feed smaller varieties infusoria. Feed larger varieties powdered food, and later add tiny worms and chopped-up midge larvae to their diet.

Silversides (Atherinidae)

Red-tailed Silverside (*Bedotia geoyi*), 6 inches (15 cm)
Geographical origin: Madagascar. **Habitat:** Fast-moving waters. **Distinguishing feature:** Surface fish.

Aquarium care: These peaceful fish swim in schools and need plenty of open areas for swimming, as well as dense plant growth along the edges and the back wall of the aquarium. Since they do not burrow, delicate, feathery plants will do well.

Water: Medium hard to hard (above 10 dH). Absolutely essential is a weekly change of water, because these fish are extremely sensitive to nitrates and to cloudy water caused by infusoria. **Temperature:** 68° to 75°F (20° to 24°C). **Food:** Live food, preferably black gnat larvae, and dry food flakes. Remember, however, that these fish will feed only at the water surface and ignore any food that sinks to the bottom. **Breeding:** The spawning period extends to several months. The fish spawn among plants, to which the eggs adhere with the aid of their threadlike

extensions. After about 1 week, the eggs hatch; the fish will not pursue their young if you make sure that the adults are well fed.

Celebes Rainbow fish (*Telmatherina ladigesi*), about 3 inches (8 cm)
Geographical origin: Southeast Asia (Celebes). **Habitat:** Fast-moving waters. **Distinguishing feature:** Surface fish.

Aquarium care: These peaceful fish swim in schools and should be kept in a large tank, about 30 inches (76 cm) or more, with plants along the edges and the back wall. Provide a cover of floating plants.

Water: Hard to very hard (above 12 dH); neutral. Absolutely essential are the addition of sea salt—1 to 2 tablespoons for each 10 quarts (liters) of water—and a weekly change of water. Transfer into water of a different chemical composition is bad for these fish; they react particularly adversely to a transfer into soft, acid water. **Temperature:** 72° to 86°F (22° to 30°C). **Food:** Live and dry food, primarily fed at the water surface. **Breeding:** If at all possible, allow morning sunlight to enter the aquarium, because it stimulates the fish to spawn. They like to spawn among plants and the root systems of the floating plant cover. The parents are vigorous predators and will go after the eggs unless you immediately remove the floating plants to which the eggs are attached. Place the plants with the eggs in a separate tank in which you can raise the hatchlings. The eggs will hatch within 8 to 11 days. Feed the young with powdered food.

Egg-laying Killifishes or Toothed Carps (Cyprinodontidae)
Photos, page 37

Geographical origin: Tropical and subtropical regions on all continents except Australia; 450 species. **Habitat:** Moving and still waters; rain puddles; usually fresh water; a few species in brackish and ocean water. **Distinguishing features:** a shape like that of the typical surface-water fish; set-back dorsal fin; undershot mouth; no lateral line on the body, but well-developed lateral line organs in the head region. **Gender difference:** Males are bright colored; females, dull. **Characteristics:** Killifishes do not usually form casual small groups. Egg-laying toothed carps (also known as killifishes) are divided into two groups, according to their reproductive methods:

Common Species of Fish

fishes that spawn on the bottom, and those that usually spawn on plants, to which the eggs adhere. The reproductive mechanism of the former group is one of the strangest known. These fish live in small rain puddles that contain water only during the rainy season. This is where the fish spawn, pressing their eggs into the bottom soil. During the dry season the puddles dry up, and all the fish die. The eggs, however, have exceptionally hard shells and survive in the mud. The eggs enter a state of arrested development to await the next rains. As soon as the rainy season comes and the eggs get wet, they hatch and the young develop into adult fish within a few months. They in turn spawn at the end of the rainy season. These killifishes are considered seasonal or annual fish because of their unusual development. In their natural habitat, their entire lifespan is no more than 8 months; even in an aquarium, they live no longer than 1½ years. Species that are not annual may grow to be 3 to 4 years old; they live in permanent waters and deposit their eggs either on plants or on the bottom. The eggs do not experience a "dry" stage, since the water does not dry out. Species that spawn on plants produce eggs that adhere to these plants. **Types suitable for an aquarium:** Most killifishes are found in Africa and South America. Various genera live in western Africa: *Aphyosemion* (may spawn either in the ground or on plants), *Roloffia* (their eggs are pressed into the ground), *Aplocheilichthys* and *Epiplatys* (both of these types spawn on plants). Most West African species have long, sometimes pike-shaped bodies, are fast swimmers, and are quite adept at jumping. Annual fishes of the genus *Nothobranchius* live in eastern and central Africa. They are somewhat plump and sluggish, with a round body. The male encircles the female with his large fins during spawning and at the same time presses the eggs into the ground with his powerful, round tail fin.

On the islands of Madagascar, the Seychelles, and others like them the species *Pachypanchax playfairi,* 4 inches (10 cm), can be found. This fish spawns and lays eggs that adhere to plants. Southeast Asia is the home of the Rice Fish (genus *Oryzias*) and species of the genus *Aplocheilus.* The Lined Panchax (*Aplocheilus lineatus*), 5 inches (12 cm), is quite a large killifish. It lives near the water surface, where it hunts and tracks its prey; it is also very aggressive toward members of its own species. Representatives of both genera (*Oryzias* and *Aplocheilus*) spawn on aquatic plants.

South America is the home of the Argentine Pearlfish (genus *Cynolebia*), *Pterolebias, Rachovia, Cynopoecilus,* and *Austrofundulus* (all of these bury their eggs in the muddy soil). *Cynolebias* varieties are shaped similarly to the African genus *Nothobranchius* (i.e., they are plump), while the other types are slender, deft swimmers. The South American Hart's Rivulus *(Rivulus hartii)* lays it eggs on plants. Southern European and Near-Eastern species like the Spanish Killifish (*Aphanius iberus*) and the Mediterranean Killifish (*Aphanius fasciatus*) live at least some of the time in brackish waters and deposit their eggs on plants.

Desert pupfishes of the genus *Cyprinodon* are found in the United States and northern Mexico. They live in more or less brackish puddles and rivulets, sometimes in hot springs, where temperatures can reach 110°F (45°C). These waters sometimes contain up to 20 percent salt, which makes them 6 times higher in salt content than seawater. These fish will spawn in and on dense growths of green algae, which also serve in part as their diet.

Aquarium care: Killifishes are recommended only for the experienced aquarium hobbyist, since their demands for top-quality water as well as for food are unusually high. To do justice to one of the species described above, you have to keep it in a separate species tank. An aquarium for killifishes does not need to be particularly large; many species can be bred in tanks holding about 5 to 10 quarts (liters) of water. You can keep these fish in a standard-sized, planted aquarium with the usual equipment and decorations, and just transfer them occasionally to a smaller tank for breeding purposes. Another option is to divide the aquarium into various regions, with one area reserved specifically for spawning. Males are known to be quite quarrelsome, and fish need plenty of hiding places among roots and rocks, in addition to the dense plant growth and abundant floating plants that make for a dimly lit tank. The bottom material should be as soft as possible and dark in color.

Water: South American, African, and East Asian species: soft; slightly acid; may be filtered over peat. European varieties: hard, requires the addition of 3 grams of sea salt per 1 quart (liter) of water. North American desert fish: hard to very hard (over 15 dH); slightly alkaline, requires the addition of 3 teaspoons of sea salt per 10 quarts (liters) of water. Frequent addition of fresh water prolongs the life of all killifishes. **Temperature:** 70° to 77°F (21° to 25°C):

Common Species of Fish

To extend the lifespan of killifishes, occasionally separate the males from the females (see "Breeding," below) and lower the water temperature to 62° to 64°F (16° to 18°C). This may allow even the annual species to survive for about 2 years. **Food:** Live food (insects, midge larvae, water fleas, various small worms) or a varied and balanced diet of freeze-dried live food and dry food. **Breeding:** Many killifishes may be bred if you carefully duplicate the natural conditions for egg development. If the fish in your tank are not among the "annuals" and their eggs adhere to plants, you can add feathery plants or an artificial nylon web to the breeding tank, and the fish will spawn almost daily. The breeding will be even more efficient and productive if you allow the parents to spawn for about 2 days, then separate them for 3 or 4 days and feed them well. This allows them to recover and delays "spawner burnout." Then start the breeding all over again. Transfer the spawn into a special tank for raising the fry, together with the water from the breeding tank. The eggs will hatch within 1 to 4 weeks.

Annual killifishes, on the other hand, need very special treatment of the eggs. This is because of their adaptation to the unpredictable environmental conditions of life in puddles of rainwater. If the rainy season begins later than usual or if a pond dries up too soon, the young hatchlings will die before they have a chance to reproduce. Therefore, some eggs need more time to develop and will not hatch until the next rain or even the next rainy season. The young fish are voracious feeders and grow rapidly; many annual killifishes are sexually mature within 3 weeks. Therefore, separate males and females as soon as you can distinguish the sexes, or the fish will spawn too soon and will quickly die.

Egg-laying toothed carps are very demanding fish. If you would like more detailed information regarding the breeding requirements of the many existing species, consult the extensive literature on this specific subject.

Live-bearing Toothed Carps (Poeciliidae)

Photos, inside front cover, page 38, and back cover

Geographical origin: Southern United States to Central and South America, to northern Argentina; imported to many other countries to control mosquitoes. **Habitat:** Slow-moving and still waters, also found in coastal regions. **Distinguishing feature:** Shape like that of other surface-water fish. **Gender differences:** Males are more colorful than females; females are larger than males. **Characteristics:** The anal fin has changed into a copulative organ, known as the gonopodium. When mating, the male inserts the gonopodium into the female and transfers a sperm packet that dissolves in the ovarian tube. Some sperm fertilize the eggs, while the remaining sperm are stored in the folds of the walls in the ovarian tubes. This ensures that subsequent eggs can be fertilized without the presence of the male. The young grow in the eggs, rich in yolk, within the female, breaking out of the eggs at the time of birth. In this way they are protected against predators and other potential environmental dangers at least until their birth. **Types suitable for an aquarium:** Among the great variety of live-bearing toothed carps, the fishes most commonly kept in aquariums belong to the genera Poecilia (-Molliensa) and Xiphophorus. The best-known live-bearer is the Guppy (Poecilia reticulata), found naturally in Central America and the northern parts of South America, and bred in many shapes and colorings. Poecilia sphenops is the ancestor of the breed known as the Black Molly, which is bred in a multitude of fin shapes. It is found in areas from Mexico to Columbia and may live in brackish waters along coastal areas. The sailfin mollies Poecilia latipinna and the slightly larger Poecilia velifera are among the mollies that inhabit brackish waters along the coastal regions of Mexico. The male of these species has an impressive dorsal fin which he likes to display by spreading it. Red and black breeds are commercially more popular and available than the green varieties found in the wild.

The Swordtail (Xiphophorus helleri), 6 inches (15 cm), is also one of the most popular of all aquarium fishes and is most frequently available commercially as one of the many red and speckled breeds, rather than the original green variety of the natural habitat. It used to be thought that Swordtails underwent a sex change, that is, that old "females" could supposedly change into sexually fertile males "if needed." Instead, it turned out that there are, in fact, two varieties of males, so-called "early" and "late" males. Indeed, the "late" males do resemble the old females in appearance. A smaller relative of the Swordtail is the Platy (Xiphophorus maculatus). There are also many breeds available of the Platy, as well as of the Variegated Platy (Xiphophorus variatus). Even though all male live-bearers are rivals, most of these species are not known for serious attacks on others.

Common Species of Fish

Aquarium care: Since live-bearing toothed carps are resistant to disease and easily satisfied, they are perfect for the novice aquarium hobbyist. They are easy to breed, even if you are inexperienced. Nevertheless, be as conscientious about their care as you are in dealing with more demanding fishes. Small live-bearers do well in an aquarium 16 inches (40 cm) long, but Swordtails and other large-finned species need a tank at least 40 inches (102 cm) in length. The larger, livelier species need an adequate swimming area, with just a few plants around the edges. Use only plants (such as *Sagittaria, Vallisneria, Elodea*) that will thrive in hard water. If you keep fishes that normally live in brackish waters, plant only giant *Vallisneria* plants. Live-bearing toothed carps like a loose cover of floating plants, because they live among such plants in their native habitat. Bottom material should be medium coarse and dark in color.

Water: Medium hard to hard; neutral to slightly alkaline; add sea salt—0.1 gram per 1 quart (liter) of water—for fishes that originate in coastal areas (e.g., *Poecilia velifera* and *P. latispinna*). Do not use peat filtering! **Temperature:** Depending on the origin of the fish, 64° to 82°F (18° to 28°C). Guppy: 64° to 73°F (18° to 23°C). Platy and Swordtails: 68° to 77°F (20° to 25°C). Sailfin Molly: 73° to 82°F (23° to 28°C). **Food:** Dry flakes and live food, especially mosquito larvae and insects, but also food from plant sources. All species like to graze on algae, and food rich in algae is particularly important for fishes from brackish waters, such as *Poecilia velifera* and *P. latipinna*. Both of these will waste away if they do not get enough algae or dry vegetable foods. Their colors will fade; their young will not grow adequately, nor is the sail-like dorsal fin likely to develop.

Breeding: Live-bearing toothed carps breed perpetually, and it is up to the aquarium owner to keep them from constantly reproducing. These fish mature sexually very quickly, and it is best to separate males and females as soon as the gonopodium begins to develop in the male. Wait until the fish are fully grown, and then select only the best male and female specimens for breeding purposes. Because the females will eat their young, remember to use a separate aquarium and to place the females in a special spawning box inside the aquarium before spawning takes place. At the time of their birth, the young will drop into the aquarium through a special opening at the bottom of the box. The fry are then out of reach of their voracious mothers. A pregnant female can be identified by the gravid spot, a darkened,

triangular pregnancy mark behind her anal fin at the back of her abdomen. In some species, the eyes of the young are already visible, prior to birth, through the female's abdomen. The young fish should be fed small live food and dry food flakes.

There are many breeds of live-bearing toothed carps. Specific standards for various shapes of fins and colorings are recognized for the Guppy, the Platy, the Swordtail, and mollies. New strains are being bred continually. All strains within a species can be cross-bred, and even hybrids can be produced by crossing certain different species. The most beautiful varieties are frequently the result of crossing the Swordtail and Platy. If you want to keep live-bearers in your community aquarium, stick with one species and one strain of this species only; randomly crossed varieties are not welcomed either by the dealer or by other aquarium hobbyists. Only hobbyists who breed cichlids will gladly accept your live-bearers as live food for their own fish. If the wild form of one species is kept together with an ornamental variety of the same species in the same aquarium, their offspring will eventually tend to revert back and resemble the wild variety more and more. The reason is that the highly bred males with their large fins move much slower than their short-finned wild counterparts; therefore, the wild males reach the females first and fertilize them. Also, if you want to breed poeciliids, be sure that the females have not yet been fertilized by males. A young female with a pregnancy mark at the time of purchase may give birth to mixed breeds of unknown origin, because one fertilization is sufficient for successive batches of eggs.

Domestically bred varieties need warm temperatures and are more demanding than the wild varieties with respect to the water quality. The exception is the Sailfin Molly; the wild strain is definitely more delicate than the cultivated variety.

Labyrinth fishes.
Above Left: Dwarf Gourami *(Colisa lalia);* above right: Siamese Fighting Fish *(Betta splendens);* middle left: Chocolate Gourami *(Sphaerichthys osphromenoides);* middle right: Combtail Paradise Fish *(Belontia signata);* below left: Blue Gourami *(Trichogaster trichopterus);* below right: Pearl Gourami *(Trichogaster leeri),* male in front, female in background.

Common Species of Fish

Sticklebacks (Gasterosteidae)
Photo, page 110

Geographical origin: Near East, North America, Europe. **Habitat:** Fresh water, brackish waters; many species are found in marine habitats. **Distinguishing features:** A spine in front of the dorsal fin that can be raised up. Brackish water species have bony plates; some freshwater species are completely naked. **Characteristics:** These fishes live in schools. The males establish specific territories during the breeding season.

Aquarium care: The Three-spined Stickleback (*Gasterosteus aculeatus*), 6 inches (15 cm), which is widely found in the Northern Hemisphere and is popular among aquarium hobbyists, should be kept in a species aquarium that has been well planted. It needs bottom sand, and plenty of hiding places in rocks and roots to enable the male to stake out and establish a particular territory and the female to find refuge after she has spawned.

Water: Low in calcium, well aerated, and well filtered. **Temperature:** Sticklebacks are cold-water fish. The temperature should not be higher than 68°F (20°C) during summer months, or 40° to 50°F (4° to 8°C) during winter months; otherwise, the females will refuse to spawn in the spring. **Food:** Live food exclusively (water fleas, worms, midge larvae, any surplus Guppies you may have). **Breeding:** During breeding season in the spring, the males begin to define their territories. The male builds a nest on the bottom, consisting of vegetation glued together with a substance secreted by his adrenal glands. He courts the round-bellied females until one of them decides to follow him to the nest. The female enters and deposits her eggs. As soon as the female leaves the nest, the male enters and fertilizes the eggs. He protects and cares for the eggs and for the young later on. A male stickleback frequently has eggs in his nest that were deposited by a series of females.

Aquarium plants.
Above left: Tape Grass *(Vallisneria spiralis);* above right: *Egeria densa;* below left: Fanwort *Cabomba caroliniana);* below right: Swordplant *(Aponogeton rigidifolius).*

Glassfishes (Centropomidae)

Geographical origin: Southeast Asia. **Habitat:** Both still and moving waters. **Distinguishing features:** Grows to 3 inches (8 cm) in length at best; is transparent: vertebrae, swim bladder, and peritoneum are clearly visible. **Gender difference:** The male's swim bladder is pointed toward the tail, while the female's is rounded. **Characteristics:** Glassfishes are peaceful, easily frightened fishes that live in groups and are also known to defend small territories.

Aquarium care: Suitable and popular for an aquarium is only one specific glassfish—the Indian Glassfish (*Chanda ranga*), 3 inches (8 cm). It is a compatible tankmate for other peaceful fishes in a community aquarium. The aquarium should be densely planted, with rocks and roots and plenty of hiding places, as well as dark-colored bottom material.

Water: A small quantity of sea salt—3 to 6 teaspoons per 10 quarts (liters)—should be added to tap water. **Temperature:** 68° to 79°F (20° to 26°C). When breeding these fishes, increase the temperature to 82°F (28°C). **Food:** Small pieces of live food, primarily water fleas and other small crustaceans. Glassfishes may accept dry food, but never use it as the exclusive diet over a long period of time. **Breeding:** Morning sunlight increases willingness to spawn. Glassfishes spawn among water plants. They do not take care of their eggs and young; raising the young is extremely difficult, because they do not hunt their own food but wait instead for food to swim to their mouths. If you attempt to breed and raise glassfishes, take care that the young are continually surrounded by a sort of "food cloud." Also, be sure to filter the aquarium water carefully.

Sunfishes (Centrarchidae)
Photo, page 110

Geographical origin: North America. **Habitat:** Peaceful, still, and clear waters with sandy bottoms; frequently among plants along the shoreline. **Distinguishing features:** Body that is flattened sideways; only one dorsal fin, with the front part of the fin equipped with hard rays and the back part with soft rays. **Types suitable for an aquarium:** Small species such as those of the genus *Enneacanthus,* 4 inches (10 cm), live in schools, except during spawning periods. Other, much larger varieties, such

Common Species of Fish

as species of *Lepomis*, 10 to 12 inches (25 to 30 cm), and *Centrarchus macropterus,* 6 inches (16 cm), are loners—they live by themselves and prey on other fish. The pygmy sunfishes, *Elassoma* species (see below) are small—2 to 3 inches (5 to 8 cm)—and make excellent cold-water aquarium subjects.

Aquarium care: Keep sunfishes in a large aquarium with plenty of domestic water plants along the edges and near the back wall. The adult fish are kept small if they are crowded or are kept in a small tank. Sunfishes need plenty of room to swim, as well as hiding places among roots, rocks, and plants. Particularly, the female needs a refuge after she has spawned because the male at that time becomes highly aggressive toward all members of his own kind. If necessary, you may have to catch the females and remove them. The bottom material should be coarse sand and fine gravel, since the fish have to be able to make spawning pits.

Water: Medium hard to hard; neutral to slightly alkaline; very clean; use a water conditioner when changing the water. The aquarium also has to be well aerated and the water well circulated, since most sunfishes need a large amount of oxygen. Remember that these fish are extremely sensitive when transferred to another tank with water of a different chemical composition. They may become covered with fungi and molds and die—all this occurring practically overnight. **Temperature:** During the summer months around 68°F (20°C), during the winter around 56° to 58°F (10° to 12°C). If you keep the temperature too high during the winter, the fish will be less energetic during the summer and some species will not spawn. **Food:** Primarily live food; also frozen and freeze-dried food once the fish are used to it. They are not especially fond of dry food flakes. **Breeding:** During spring and summer, at the time of their spawning period, males are very territorial and manage to fan the sand until they have built large pits, generally between plants or rocks. Some species even reinforce the pits with vegetation. During spawning, females are colored more brightly than the males. Right after spawning, the female takes off without so much as a glance at her new brood. The eggs mix with the grains of sand and form batches of spawn, which the male cares for and fans. Even after the eggs have hatched, the male continues to watch over the young, protecting his small group of hatchlings, and has been known to "put the young to bed" in the spawning pits.

Everglades Pygmy Sunfish
(*Elassoma evergladei*) and
Banded Pygmy Sunfish (*E. zonatum*)
Geographical origin: Florida.

Aquarium care: Pygmy sunfishes are quite different, both in size and in behavior, from all other sunfishes. They can be kept in tanks 16 to 20 inches (41 to 51 cm) long.

Water: Medium hard; neutral to slightly alkaline. **Temperature:** The native habitat is the southeastern United States. During the summer months 77° to 86°F (25° to 30°C); during the winter months 56° to 58°F (10° to 12°C) (to encourage the fish to spawn in the spring). **Food:** Live food, algae (important!), occasionally dry food. **Breeding:** The males do not build spawning nests, and the couple spawn at random on plants. During the spawning period, the male is more colorful than the female. Both male and female ignore the eggs and young, once they have spawned.

Archerfishes (Toxotidae)
Photo, page 110

Geographical origin: Tropical western parts of Asia to Australia. **Habitat:** Fresh water, brackish waters, marine waters. **Distinguishing feature:** Archerfishes (e.g., *Toxotes jaculator*) have developed a highly unusual method of getting food (see drawing, page 97): they spit a well-aimed stream of water at an insect on a plant above the water, thus "shooting" it down, and then devour it.

Aquarium care: Archerfishes of similar size do well together, but larger species are often quite aggressive toward smaller varieties. These fishes may grow to 8 inches (20 cm) in length and therefore need a large tank that is well planted and provides plenty of hiding places.

Water: Medium hard. **Temperature:** 75° to 82°F (24° to 28°C). **Food:** Exclusively live food, primarily large insects. Remember that these fish will accept only food that is fed from the water surface.

Leaffishes (Nandidae)

Geographical origin: South America, West Africa, southern Asia. **Habitat:** Jungle waters. **Characteristics:** Mostly small, up to 4 inches (10 cm), with large heads and highly protrusible mouths. Thorny dorsal

Common Species of Fish

fins highly developed. **Distinguishing features:** *Monocirrhus polyacanthus* is a 3½-inch (9-cm) variety, well-known for its remarkable mimicry of a floating leaf in the water. It swims with its head down in a slowly tumbling, spinning fashion, by which it approaches its prey. Once close, it opens its giant mouth quickly and sucks in the unsuspecting victim.

Types suitable for an aquarium: *Monocirrhus polyacanthus; Nandus nandus,* approx. 8 inches (20 cm); *Polycentrus Schomburgki,* approx. 4 inches (10 cm). They are all inconspicuous and dark colored.

Aquarium Care: The Nandidae need large, well-planted tanks. They eat all fishes of up to three-fourths their own size, and should, therefore, be kept only in artistic show tanks.

Water: *Monocirrhus* needs soft, lightly acid water (2 to 4 dH, pH 6 to 6.5). *Nandus* and *Polycentrus* need hard or medium-hard water, lightly acid. Nandids need 1 to 2 teaspoons of sea salt added per 2½ gallons of water. **Temperature:** 75° to 79°F (24° to 26°C); for breeding, about 86°F (30°C). **Food:** Live food, exclusively in the form of fish. The amount required equals that of the nandids' own body weight. **Breeding:** Most leaffishes deposit their eggs on carefully cleaned plant leaves; *Polycentrus* places its eggs on leaves or in caves. Among most *Nandus* varieties the male cares for eggs and young, except for *Nandus nandus,* which disperses its transparent eggs all over the ground and leaves them uncared for by either male or female parents.

Cichlids (Cichlidae)

Photos, front cover, pages 81 and 82, and back cover

Geographical origin: Approximately 160 genera with more than 900 species: about 700 in Africa, about 200 in Central and South America; 2 only in India. **Habitat:** Most cichlids inhabit the still regions of shorelines in lakes and rivers, especially where undergrowth, roots, and stones provide plenty of hiding places. Some types live along coastal rock regions of large lakes, but none can survive on sand or rocks unless there are some types of hiding places.

Characteristics: The dorsal fin has bony rays in front, soft rays in back. Most cichlids have the standard fish shape, with only a few variations: an elongated body type (*Crenicichla julidochromis*) and a compressed, disc-shaped form (*Symphysodon, Pterophyl-lum, Mesonanta*). All of these have large heads. Old males develop a fat-storage hump on their foreheads. Aquarium varieties are usually between 7 and 18 inches (18 and 46 cm) in length.

Distinguishing feature: All cichlids perform some sort of brood care.

In *open brood care,* thousands of small, transparent or protectively colored eggs are deposited openly on stones or plants. Males and females look quite alike; they court each other and share the territorial defense; both clean the substrates chosen for the egg deposits and take care of the young. In many varieties the male and female continue their partnership after the breeding season is finished. Most fishes in this category live naturally in nutrient-rich muddy or cloudy waters where microorganisms abound to feed the young offspring. Spawning occurs mostly during the rainy season, when rivers carry a rich variety of nutrients from flooded lands. This is particularly true of favorite places like sun-bathed shallow waters over extensively flooded valleys or riverbanks. Some of the most common cichlids of this type are the Firemouth (*Cichlasoma meeki*), approx. 15 inches (38 cm); Zebra (*C. nigrofasciatum*), 7 inches (18 cm); many of the genus *Aequidens;* and species of *Tilapia.* Other open-brood-care species are the Deep Angelfish—*Pterophyllum scalare,* 7 inches (18 cm); and the discus fishes—*Symphysodon aequifasciata* and *S. discus,* about 14 inches (36 cm).

Hidden brood care is characterized by larger but fewer eggs. Some varieties hide their fry in caves; others carry them in their mouths until the young can fend for themselves. Males in this group are larger and more distinctively colored than females. These fishes pair only for the purpose and the duration of the breeding season. Usually females are solely responsible for the brood care.

Cave brooders and mouthbrooders are the two main groups of brood hiders. *Cave brooders* consist mainly of harem breeding groups, which form as soon as the male has fought for a territory. The females within a harem group are frequently quite aggressive. Spawning takes place inside caves, and subsequently the female assumes all of the brood-care responsibilities. The male continues to defend the territory alone unless a large prey fish appears, at which time the female and the young help with the defense. The young of several varieties, such as *Lamprologus brichardi* and the *Julidochromis* genus, help the males with territorial defense as well as with the supervision of still younger fish.

Common Species of Fish

Mouthbrooders have developed among several highly specialized groups of cichlids. The East African waters, specifically the lakes Tanganyika and Malawi, are homes to the genera *Haplochromis, Tropheus, Pseudotropheus, Labeotropheus,* and *Autonocara,* as well as some *Tilapia* varieties. These fishes form pairs only for breeding purposes. Males form colonies in shallow waters, where each of them digs a spawning pit and jealously defends it until a female arrives to deposit her fry. The male tries to attract the female while she is swimming close to his territory. The female follows the male to his spawning pit, where she deposits some of the eggs. These eggs will be fertilized either at this time or after the female has scooped them up into her mouth. Some African varieties have developed a sort of egg decoy: *Haplochromis* varieties show it in the form of large, round yellow-orange spots on the anal fins, while *Tilapia* males have developed grapelike appendages around the genital papilla that simulate eggs. The latter structures attract the female closely to the genital opening of the male, from which the female then sucks in the necessary sperm. Subsequently the females leave these colonies with their fertilized eggs in their mouths. After about 1 week the young hatch inside the mother's mouth. Even after they leave for the open water, they will return for safety when they feel threatened. Whereas the mouth-brooding females are inconspicuously colored like sand, the males of these colony dwellers are magnificently decorated.

Some types of mouthbrooders live along the rocky coastal banks of lakes. In these *Tropheus, Pseudotropheus, Labetropheus,* and *Haplochromis* groups, male and female fish live together in small colonies or in loosely organized schools over extensive territories. Individual fish, however, defend their individual feeding territories, which also include their hiding places. Males and females have equal environmental requirements; they look alike, and their behavioral patterns are similar except for hierarchical differences: highly ranked females look like males; lowly ranked males, like females. Simulated egg spots are found on both sexes, but those of males are usually larger. Spawning and fertilization behavior are the same as those of male colony dwellers. However, individual breeding spots are not necessary, and some *Tropheus* species deposit their eggs in open waters. These eggs are so large and rich in yolk that mouthbrooding can proceed for 4 weeks without the necessity to feed the young.

In less specialized forms of mouthbrooders, behavioral patterns range from totally unprotected egg deposits in open waters to highly elaborate hiding behavior. Most of these fishes originate from lakes in central and western Africa and in South America. The name of the South American genus *Geophagus* means "dirt-eating." All species of *Geophagus* are characterized by monogamous pairs, and the partners look alike. Eggs are deposited on stones. *Geophagus brasiliensis* leaves its eggs to develop in open water, while *G. sarinamensis* and *G. jurupari* fan and clean their eggs for days until they take them in their mouths ready to hatch or already in the larval stage. *Geophagus hondae* parents scoop their eggs up into their mouths right after depositing them. The genus *Gymnogeophagus* is closely related to *Geophagus.* These fishes also deposit their eggs on stones; however, the females alone pick the young up into their mouths for brood care, and lead them around in the territory. In the West African species *Chromidotilapia finleyi,* mouthbrooding is shared by males and females, each taking a day's turn at a time. In other species of *Chromidotilapia,* however, the male alone carries the eggs in his mouth. This group forms lasting pairs, and male and female look very much alike. There are also mouthbrooders among the South American genus *Aequidens;* males and females take turns in the care of the young. *Sarotherodon (-Tilapia) melanotherodon* from West Africa has specialized mouthbrooding care, developed only by the males.

Aquarium care: Most cichlids are not compatible in a beautifully planted community tank with live-bearing toothed carps, barbs, or salmonids. Frequently, however, angelfishes are kept in community tanks, and sometimes dwarf cichlids (*Apistogramma*) and also king cichlids (*Pelviachromis*). None of these, however, does very well in this mixed company, and these fishes won't multiply successfully. The problem is not that they endanger other, smaller fishes, but rather that they suffer from the continuous motion of school fishes, and they do not take well to the harder water in which live-bearing fishes are kept. Until cichlid needs became better defined, these fishes used to be kept in tanks that were too small and too crowded. Because they had to fight competitors for food and territory, they were considered ruffians; and when they dug little sand holes to protect their young, they uprooted plants and "rearranged" decorative rock formations, which subsequently collapsed. Because of their behavioral characteristics cichlids belong in an aquarium tank that holds at least 75 gallons (284 liters)—but a larger tank is better. Even the small cichlids need plenty of floor space, since they live in harems and colonies.

The most important components in a cichlid aquarium are large stone structures in which lower ranked animals can hide. These stone structures must be placed square on the tank floor to prevent the fish from undermining them by their digging behavior. East African mouthbrooders enjoy elaborate rocky constructions. The open-water brooders require some vertical flat stones, and also some flat stones lying on the bottom on which to leave their fry. Cave brooders will gladly accept parts of flower pots or coconut shells. The more cave formations you offer them, the more successfully they will breed for you. Cichlids from jungle waters, especially discus fishes, angelfishes, and *Cichlasoma* species, will greatly appreciate abundant root formations in which they can hide. The bottom in the cichlid tank should not be too roughly grained. A sandy layer a little more than ½ inch deep is enough for the fish to dig their necessary spawning holes.

Large cichlids do not require plants in their tanks. Sometimes sturdy plants along the territorial borders will survive; since eggs are deposited in the center of the territories, the peripheral plants may (or may not) escape uprooting. Another possibility is the use of potted plants covered by pebbles. Plant-eating cichlids will often spare Java ferns and the hard-leaved *Cryptocoryne* plants as long as sufficient lettuce and dried plant foods are provided. Cichlids are grateful for some floating plant cover, since they become skittish if the light is too strong. In particular, the jungle-derived fishes, especially discus fishes, love soft, dimmed lighting.

It is best to keep mouthbrooding pairs together, and to group harem-forming cave brooders by placing a large male with a group of small females. In tanks with the highly specialized mouthbrooding fishes, it is also recommended to add several females for one male, because a male can kill a single female through overzealous courtship when the female is not ready for breeding. If there are several females, the male aggression will be more tolerably distributed over all the females.

In an aquarium shop it is not at all easy to find male and female pairs, or groups of females with one male, when you look into a crowded tank that may be full of young fish and of adults that look all alike.

Although the characteristically elongated dorsal and anal fins may help you to find young males, this is not always the case. Therefore, you are bound to end up buying more young fish than you need, just to give your aquarium inhabitants a chance to grow and mature, at which time one or a few aggressive males will chase away all competitors. It is best to know in advance who will take your unwanted fish off your hands, since most aquarium dealers will not take them back. In any event, you should have a spare aquarium tank ready to be set up, since there will be other occasions, such as biting incidents, when you will need an isolation tank. This spare tank should be equipped with all necessary technical accessories for immediate use.

Most adult cichlids are fairly aggressive. In larger groups these fish will establish a ranking order: the strongest fish, usually the biggest male, dominates all the other fish in the tank, the second largest chases all those smaller than himself, and so forth. The smallest fish may be chased to exhaustion and death. Death may also conclude a fight between equally strong males competing for territory or for a female. This type of unfortunate emergency occurs typically only in an aquarium setting. In their natural habitat fish withdraw after short fighting incidents; there is no lack of space as in an aquarium, where the weaker fish must remain continually within reach of the stronger territorial owner. This space problem is responsible for the deaths of many newcomers to aquariums: the new fish, still frightened from its environmental change and transport, tries to hide in a cave and, in doing so, invades an already owned territory. The owner will chase the newcomer away, right into another owner's hiding place, and so on, until the exhausted fish ends up at the water surface in one corner, gasping for air, and attacked by others from below. Should such a situation occur, you must remove the new fish immediately, since a few minutes' delay may mean its death.

If you must add a single new fish to an established group of cichlids, proceed as follows: remove all the fish, take out and rearrange all the rock formations, and exchange some of the water; then place the new fish in the tank first, follow with the smallest of the established group, and add the others in order of size, the largest last. This procedure can be neglected only if the new fish is larger than all of the old fish in the tank. When you remove all the fish from your cichlid tank, be sure to place each fish in a separate container. This is especially important with the

Common Species of Fish

pugnacious mouthbrooding cichlids from lakes Tanganyika and Malawi of East Africa (e.g., the African Jewelfish).

Water: South and Central American cichlids, (*Aequidens, Apistogramma, Cichlasoma, Crenicichla, Geophagus, Pterophyllum*) require soft and slightly acid water, which should be peat-filtered for *Apistogramma* and for *Crenicichla* species. Discus fishes, from the Amazon region, are used to soft (3 dH), acid (pH 6.5) water. *Pelviachromis* species need the addition of sea salt to their water. Medium-hard and hard water with a low alkaline pH is needed for East African cichlids (*Astatotilapia, Aulonocara, Eretmodos, Haplochromis* mouthbrooders, and various *Lamprologus* types). Cichlids from India require brackish water with strong filtration and frequent changes. Large cichlids, like the pearl cichlids, which reach about 12 inches (30 cm) in length, are voluminous eaters and need to have at least one-third of their water changed weekly. Since ammonium is not formed from ammonia in alkaline water, you must also frequently change the water of East African inhabitants. To prevent the accumulation of by-products from chemical changes of nitrogen compounds, you can either use sophisticated hydrocultured plants, for which you must purchase specific filtered growth containers, or try simply a philodendron, which functions through its air-root system. Discus fishes and larger cichlids need one-fourth of the tank water changed every 3 weeks. Dwarf cichlids like *Apistogramma* and *Papiliochromis* cannot tolerate any traces of heavy metals in the water, necessitating chemical water treatment at each change. **Temperature:** Close to 80°F (27°C). For breeding tanks, increase the temperature 2° or 3°F. **Food:** Live food, food flakes, food pellets. For small cichlids under 8 inches (20 cm) and for most mouthbrooders, the live food can consist of waterfleas, *Tubifex* worms, or chopped earthworms or brine shrimp. Larger cichlids get cleaned earthworms, insect larvae, shredded fish, brine shrimp, chopped or shredded beef heart, baby guppies, or mollies. Herbivorous cichlids are fed clean, fresh lettuce and dried plant food pellets. **Breeding:** Most cichlids multiply freely as long as their nutrition and environment are maintained correctly. With some cichlids, however, breeding is not easy; you need knowledge and experience to succeed with discus fishes, *Uaru*, some dwarf cichlids like *Cichlasoma,* and *Apistogramma*. Much information can be found in the widely available literature on cichlids.

Labyrinth Fishes and Climbing Perches
(Anabantidae)
Photos, page 127 and back cover

Geographical origin: Most species from Southeast Asia and India, a few from Africa. **Habitat:** Rivers, creeks, and ponds with dense plant growth. Asian varieties are also found in flooded rice fields, sewage-plant ponds, and irrigation ditches. Some species live in fast-flowing rivers. **Characteristics:** Most fishes in this group are relatively deep bodied, but a few have elongated shapes with a rounded cross-section. Most Asian varieties are surface dwellers, while African types are more likely to be midzone oriented. The dorsal and anal fins usually have hard, long, pointed spines. The pelvic fins of *Trichogaster, Trichopsis,* and *Colisa* species have evolved into threadlike sensory organs for feeling, smelling, and tasting. **Distinguishing feature:** The labyrinth fishes have a unique accessory breathing apparatus—the labyrinth—which allows them to live in as oxygen-poor waters as sewage ponds. This breathing organ is so well developed that many varieties of these fishes have reduced gill-breathing capacities and must breathe air; otherwise they will drown. The African varieties are not as dependent on airbreathing as are the Asian types. The Kissing Gourami (*Helostoma temmincki*), 20 inches (30 cm), uses its gills to feed because of the modified gill arches, which can filter plankton. Young labyrinth fishes breathe solely through gills until, some weeks later, their breathing labyrinth chambers have developed.

Aquarium care: Many labyrinth fishes are ideally suited for community tanks, especially in the company of quiet bottom dwellers. They can, however, be impatient toward their own kind, especially during nest-building periods. With the exception of the most aggressive of the fighting fishes, *Betta splendens,* 2½ inches (6 cm) and some smaller *Betta* varieties, as well as the Paradisefish (*Macropodus opercularis*), 4 inches (10 cm) and the Climbing Perch (*Anabas testudineus*), about 8 inches (20 cm), which is not a true perch), most labyrinth fishes are very peaceful. The African and the Asian species listed above should be kept in groups of equal-sized fish or varieties large enough not to be swallowed. The size of the tank must fit the size of the fish it will house. Fighting fishes and gouramis need tanks at least 30 inches (76 cm) long; the larger varieties require 36 inches (91 cm) or more. Smaller tanks are adequate for small varieties like the Dwarf Gourami (*Colisa* *chuna)* and *C. lalia,* both about 2 inches (5 cm), as well as the Croaking Gourami (*Trichopsis vittatus*), about 3 inches (8 cm). The fighting fish, especaily *Betta splendens,* need tanks with at least 4 gallons (15 liters) of water—the more the better, particularly if you want two males in the same tank. Unless the tank is very large and well stocked with plants and fish, two males will fight each other to death, although sometimes males will get along if they have grown up together. Each male fighting fish must have enough space to build a territory. These fish start fighting for social rank order when they are very young and only about ½ inch (1¼ cm) long. This order will subsequently be respected by the individual fishes.

The labyrinth fishes require a relatively low tank. To breed the larger gourami varieties, you should, in fact, lower the water level to 6 or 8 inches (15 or 20 cm). The type of bottom material is quite unimportant for these fishes, since they spend most of their life as surface dwellers. In general, the bottom area should be kept dark, except for some species that prefer dimmed lighting, for example, *Macropodus cupanus* and *M. dayi,* both 3 inches (8 cm); the Pearl Gourami (*Trichogaster leeri*), 4 to 6 inches (10 to 15 cm); and the genus *Ctenopoma.*

Since all of these varieties need many hiding places, it is essential that you provide dense plant growth along the edges and the backwall. If hiding places are scarce, the male may chase a female to death after she has deposited the eggs. Floating plants make bubble-nest building much easier (see Breeding, below). Roots, stones, and caves made from coconut shells or rocks are also very useful. Most labyrinth fishes prefer quiet, calm water. Only the pugnacious Fighting Fish (*Betta pugnax*), rarely kept in aquariums, requires water with a strong current. An excellent tank cover is mandatory to prevent the air over the water surface from cooling below the water temperature. Cool air will chill the fish, usually with fatal results. The Climbing Perch (*Anabas testudineus*) needs a good tank cover because of its jumping ability. In its natural environment this fish is able to move with astonishing speed on land: it hooks its toothed gill covers in the ground, supports its body by its pectoral fins, and pushes forward with the help of the caudal fin. If you own Climbing Perches, you should remember to count them daily. If one of these fish gets out of the tank, it won't just lie on the floor—it will run away before you discover the loss. If not quickly discovered, the fish will soon die from dehydration unless the floor is very humid, in which case the Climbing Perch could survive for up to 2 days.

Water: Soft to medium hard; close to neutral; most varieties have modest requirements in regard to water quality. The tiny *Colisa* varieties need peat-filtered, soft water for breeding. Supplemental peat is also advantageous for African bushfish varieties, the Croaking Gourami, and especially the Chocolate Gourami (*Spaerichthys osphromenoides*), about 2½ inches (6 cm). All labyrinth fishes do better with frequent water changes. **Temperature:** 72 to 83°F (22 to 28°C); 86°F (30°C) for breeding. Only *Macropodus* species can tolerate some periods in water temperatures below 69°F (20°C). **Food:** Flakes or live food; these fish prefer mosquitoes, fleas, and other small invertebrates. The larger fish need larger food, such as insect larvae or even small fish. Brine shrimp may be needed for the smallest varieties. The young can feed on infusoria or brine-shrimp eggs. Frozen and freeze-dried foods are generally also accepted by most labyrinth fishes. **Breeding:** In most species brood care is taken over by the males. Many varieties, including the gouramis, *Betta, Colisa,* the threadfishes, and *Macropodus,* originate from very quiet waters, and these build bubble nests in the aquarium. The males start to build the bubble nests about 1 or 2 days before spawning. Bubbles are formed by taking air into the mouth, mixing it with a sticky secretion, and then spitting the mixture out, thereby causing bubbles to form, rise to the surface, and stick together in clumps. Then the male attracts a female into the space below the nest, where he turns her upside down. As she deposits the eggs, he fertilizes them. Most of the eggs float up into the bubbles. The male then picks up with his mouth any sinking eggs before they touch the bottom, and spits them into the bubble nest. This procedure is repeated until the female has deposited all her eggs, at which time the male chases her away. He then remains underneath the bubble nest for an average of 2 to 3 days. During this time, he repairs bubbles, picks up sinking eggs, and stands guard. The young hatch and stay in the nest until they have used up their yolk-sac nutrients. When any of them get out of the nest, the male proceeds as he did with the eggs, and spits them back into place. When the yolk has been consumed, the young fish swim out of the nest, and their father pays no further attention to their whereabouts.

Fishes from fast-flowing rivers cannot use bubble nests for breeding. These varieties, of which the

Common Species of Fish

mouth brooding Fighting Fish (*Betta pugnax*) is an example, proceed as follows: the male receives the eggs with his anal fin for fertilization; from there the female picks them up and "spits" them into the male's mouth, where they stay until they hatch. The Chocolate Gourami (*Sphaerichthys asphrome-noides*) breeds both ways, depending on native location. The varying origins make it difficult to pair these gouramis, since it is often impossible to learn their true origins from the pet shop owner.

There are also cave-breeding varieties of labyrinth fishes—for example, *Parosphromenus deissneri*. The African varieties do not usually build bubble nests; most of these spawn in open water or among plants; examples are *Ctenopoma kingsleyae*, 8 in. (20 cm); *C. maculatum; C. muieri*; the Kissing Gourami, and the Climbing Perch. The eggs of these fish have a high oil content, which causes them to float to the water surface.

Gobies and Sleepers (Gobiidae)

Geographical origin: Worldwide. **Habitat:** Mainly oceans, rarely brackish or fresh waters. **Characteristics:** Typical bottom-feeder structures. Pelvic fins usually fused, and suction cups formed to adhere to the ground surfaces.

Aquarium care: Southeast Asian varieties (e.g., *Brachygobius xantocona* and other species of this genus) are suitable for the aquarium. Although they grow to only about 2 inches (4.5 to 5 cm), they behave territorially toward their own kind. The aquarium needs all kinds of hiding places, such as stones, roots, flower pots, and coconut shells. The bottom layer must be dark colored. Plants must tolerate saline conditions. These fish are no candidates for community tanks.

Water: Hard or very hard (20 to 30 dH); alkaline (pH 7.5 to 8.5); thorough filtration; 1 to 2 teaspoons sea salt per 2½ gallons of water. **Temperature:** 75° to 85°F (24° to 29°C). **Food:** Small live food. **Breeding:** Adding fresh water and increasing the temperature will stimulate spawning. Egg-bearing females appear quite fat compared to males. The spawn is deposited under rocks and in caves. Males perform brood care.

Spiny Eels (Mastacembilidae)
Photo, page 64

Geographical origin: South and Southeast Asia, tropical Africa. **Habitat:** Quiet, densely overgrown waters with sandy or muddy bottoms; fresh and brackish waters. **Characteristics:** Eel-like or ropelike shape; long, mobile, snoutlike, undershot mouth. The dorsal, caudal, and anal fins are fused into a single continuous fin. There are a few individual, erectable, spiny rays right in front of the soft dorsal fin. Most species have no pelvic fins at all. **Distinguishing features:** The eel-like varieties dig themselves in during the day, with only mouths and eyes protruding from the sandy bottom; the rope-shaped fish hide between plants and rocks. During the night both types emerge to search for worms, insect larvae, tiny crustaceans, and smaller fish.

Aquarium care: The spiny eels are exceptionally intelligent fish that get to know their keeper quickly and turn into veritable pets. Toward their own kind, however, they are often belligerent; sometimes they will attack fish of another genus also. The largest species of these eels, the red-striped *Mastacembelus erythrotaenia*, 3 feet (1 meter), feeds mainly on fish. Spiny eels are best kept in a densely planted tank with a soft, sandy bottom. Many hiding places and caves are needed, and the illumination must be kept dimmed through floating plants.

Water: Hard or medium hard; neutral pH; 1 to 2 teaspoons of salt per 2½ gallon of water. Frequent addition of fresh water is mandatory. **Temperature:** 71° to 84°F (22° to 28°C). **Food:** Live food, mainly worms, insect larvae, and fish. Dry flakes are not welcome, but spiny eels do get used to frozen and freeze-dried live food, as well as to some food pellets. Feeding should be scheduled for the late evening just before the lights are turned off. **Breeding:** These fish have now been bred successfully in an aquarium setting. The large male *Mastacembelus pancalus* trails the female and then sniffs around her ventral fins until, finally, the two fish embrace with their fins and spawn at the water surface among *Riccia* plant beds. The parents do not guard their fry. The young hatch after 3 days, remaining in the plant bed. After about 3 more days they swim free, feed on eggs of brine shrimp, and grow to a little more than 1 inch (3 cm) before they begin living on the bottom of the aquarium.

Common Species of Fish

Puffers (Tetraodontidae)

Geographical origin: Tropics and subtropics.
Habitat: Mainly oceans; rarely fresh or brackish
waters. **Characteristics:** Bowling-pin-shaped body;
large head with large eyes set far apart; teeth fused
into a sharp wedge. The fused teeth have evolved to
facilitate feeding on clams and snails. **Distinguishing
features:** Unlike other fish, the puffers use their
pectoral fins for all forward and backward motion;
the caudal fin is used only as a rudder. Each pectoral
fin can move independently in several directions,
giving these fish exceptional agility. Another peculiarity
is the stomach, which is larger than usual and takes
up either water or air. This unique feature allows
a puffer to turn into a ball-like shape when danger
lurks, so that its enemy would need a giant mouth to
be able to swallow it. While these fish inflate themselves, they can croak, and they can spit water. Puffers
are venomous. Their poison, tetrogonin, is produced
by the gonads and deposited in several organs.

Types suitable for an aquarium: From Southeast
Asia, for freshwater aquariums: *Carinotetraodon
somphongsi,* 8 inches (20 cm); *Tetraodon fluviatilis,*
also called the Green Puffer, 6 to 7 inches (18 cm)
(see color photo, back cover, below left); and *T.
palembangensis,* 8 inches, (20 cm). From Africa: the
African Leopard Puffer *(T. schoutedeni).*

   Aquarium care: Most kinds quickly turn tame.
Because of their territorial behavior, they are best
kept in large show tanks decorated with plants, roots,
and rock formations that serve as hiding places.

Plenty of space for unhindered swimming is mandatory. The Leopard Puffer is not as aggressive as the
others and can, therefore, be tried in a community
aquarium. If you keep any varieties that originate
in brackish water, remember to choose plants that
will tolerate this kind of water.

   Water: For *Tetraodon somphongsi* and *T. palembangensis:* soft or medium hard; slightly acid to
neutral. For *T. fluviatilis:* hard or medium hard;
neutral pH, with sea salt. For *T. schoutedeni:* medium
to hard; neutral pH, without sea salt. A puffer aquarium
must have a top-quality filter because these fish are
exceedingly sensitive to nitrogen compounds,
especially ammonia. **Temperature:** 75° to 85°F (24°
to 28°C). **Food:** Mainly snails and clams (puffers
are sometimes added to an aquarium to rid it of snail
infestation), also worms, insect larvae, small crustaceans. Food pellets are accepted. Clams and snails
must be added no matter what the main food is,
because they serve to sharpen the dental ridge. The
tamer fish will chew on cuttle bone when you hold it
in the water. **Breeding:** Spawning behavior is
diverse; open water, as well as substrates, is used for
brooding. The Green Puffer spawns on stones. Males
provide brood care. Frequently, the males hover
over the fry until tadpole-like young hatch from the
eggs; these are then closely guarded by the males.
The Congo Puffer (*Tetraodon schoutedeni*) spawns
on leaves and also in open water, with no brood care
provided. The male fertilizes the eggs by biting the
female's ventral area and clinging to her until all eggs
have been deposited and fertilized. The genus
Carinatetraodon spawns in open water.

Books for Further Information

Braemer, H. and Scheurmann, I. *Tropical Fish*. New York: Barron's. 1983.

Maryland, Hans. J. *Complete Home Aquarium*. New York: Putnam Pub. Group. 1981.

Pinter, H. *Labyrinth Fish*. New York: Barron's. 1986.

Scheurmann, Ines. *Water Plants in the Aquarium*. New York: Barron's. 1987.

Index

Index

Index

Index

Index

Index

Photo credits

Kahl: Inside front cover, inside back cover, page 9;
page 10 middle left, middle right, below left; page 20
above left, below right; page 38 below left, below
right; page 63 middle left, middle right, below left,
below right; page 99 below left; page 100 above left,
below right; page 127 above left, below right; back
cover (middle left, middle right).
König: Page 10 above right; page 37 middle right;
page 38 above right.
Paffrath: Page 109; page 128.
Reinhard: Front cover; page 10 above left; pages 19
and 20 above right, middle left, middle right, below
left; page 37 above left, above right, middle left, below
left, below right; page 38 above left, middle left,
middle right; page 63 above left, above right, pages 64
and 81; page 82; page 99 above left, above right,
below right; page 100 above right, middle left, middle
right, below left; page 110; page 127 above right,
middle left, middle right, below left, back cover
(above left, above middle, above right, below left,
below right).